Jetway Joshua
(aka Carl Lewis Lodjic)

Jetway Joshua
(aka Carl Lewis Lodjic)

Four Score and Twenty

Carl Lodjic

Writers Club Press
San Jose New York Lincoln Shanghai

Jetway Joshua (aka Carl Lewis Lodjic)
Four Score and Twenty

Writers Club Press
an imprint of iUniverse.com, Inc.

For information address:
iUniverse.com, Inc.
5220 S 16th, Ste. 200
Lincoln, NE 68512
www.iuniverse.com

ISBN: 0-595-15192-2

Printed in the United States of America

Dedicated to my dear sweet Nena (Virginia)

without whom I could not have survived.

Content

Foreword

The life of Carl Lewis Lodjic (Jetway Joshua) from birth in the ghetto of Watts, California; through, at age six, the death of his father from lead poisoning due to spray painting Navy ships with red lead, in the Long Beach, California shipyard.

He saw that he had to help his mother, because she had four kids to provide for; so he got a two-hundred customer newspaper route, which he delivered on roller skates, since they couldn't afford a bicycle. He also got a job making hamburgers at the concessions stand in the Alhambra City Park; and hired on as helper to a milkman who served the "millionaires" homes in Pasadena at the time of the Stock Market crash.

At nineteen he got a job with a large structural steel fabricating company in Lynwood, California; where he climbed the ladder from lowest paid flunky to becoming the principal owner and C.E.O., and where he created the Jetway airline passenger loading systems.

Following the death of his wife of fifty-two years to a brain surgeons error, he entered a four year trip into perdition.

He is now living on "cloud nine" in Boulder City, Nevada with his beautiful sweet Nena.

Virginia Lee Chacon-Hamilton

Score 1

In the beginning; after reading about the Margaret Sanger Birth Control Clinic in New York, Mom decided she wanted another child. But she didn't approve of "planned" birth control, so I arrived in our home in the ghetto of Watts, California on May 9, 1917 at 1:07am.

I had stinging drops put in my eyes, was hung by my feet, and slapped on my bottom; then I had something soft and juicy pushed into my mouth.

I was not yet an hour old, and I knew all there was to know about eating. The lady feeding me was soft and pretty, and had curly blonde hair.

Mom later told me that when I was born our house had three other people: my two-year old brother, my dad, and my grandpa. It was Grandpa's house because we couldn't afford one of our own.

Grandpa was too old to work, and Dad was busy earning a living for all of us.

Mom showed me to my brother Rolly, who didn't like the competition. He wanted Mom to put me back where I came from.

Mom's family, Grandma and Grandpa Sager, had lived in New York; and Dad's family, Grandma and Grandpa Lodjic, had lived in South Dakota.

Dad met Mom in New York when he was riding in a rodeo. It was "love at first sight", and they married in Brooklyn.

California seemed to be the place to earn a living and to have a good climate, so they moved to Watts. Dad found that they didn't need comboys there, so he got a job in Long Beach painting Navy ships with red lead.

Mexican Annie, the midwife down the street came to our house twice, and each time she shut herself in the bedroom with Mom, and came out with a baby.

Mom called the first one Dorothy, and the second one she called Bernice.

They were both cute; but they were girls, so they wouldn't be any fun.

Dad was my hero and I was his "curiosity kid", he smoked cigars and I wanted to be just like him so I watched carefully; he took one from the box by his chair and took off a little paper ring, then bit off a little piece of the small end and spit it into his hand. He licked the end and put it in his mouth, and lit a match and put it to the other end and sucked on it. He blew out smoke and said "aah".

When Dad was at work and Mom was busy in the kitchen, I went over to the box by his chair and took out a cigar and some matches. I crawled under the dining table where I was hidden by the long table cloth that came all the way to the floor, and did all the things I saw Dad do. I put the lit match to the end and sucked real hard and started to say "aah" but choked instead.

Mom must have heard me choke because she came into the dining room and picked up one corner of the tablecloth, waved some of the smoke away, and said, "I hope you get darn good and sick." She dropped the cloth and went back in the kitchen. I never knew what "darn good" meant, but sure found out about sick. That was my last cigar.

One day I saw Grandpa Lodjic dig a deep hole in the back yard, and put some live baby kittens in it and fill it with water and dirt. He pounded down the dirt with his shovel. I was mad. I didn't like him, but Mom said I had to put up with him because he lived with us in his house. He was just an ornery old man, with tobacco juice in his chin whiskers who was too old to work; but since Dad wasn't paid very much, we had to live with him.

When it was time for me to start school Mom put my sisters, Dorothy and Bernice, in the baby buggy and walked me about a mile up the alley to St. Aloysius School where I started in the first grade. Rolly had gone on ahead because he was a grown-up second grader.

Sister Evangel was my teacher. She told us kids, "Don't talk, wiggle, look around the room, or make any noise. Just sit still, be quiet, and pay attention! If you need to go to the bathroom hold up one finger; and when I nod to you, it's allright for you to go."

She had no sooner mentioned it than I did need to go, but I'd be embarrassed if the other kids knew it; so I held it and squirmed, but soon knew I could hold it no longer.

I held up my finger and Sister looked right at me but didn't nod. I squirmed and waved my finger around and around. Nothing from Sister! Again she looked right at me but acted like she didn't see me. I was about to lose it, and that would be awful, so I jumped up and ran out of the room and down the hall to "the boys".

I went, I washed, and I ran back to my desk.

Sister always looked "scowly" so I couldn't tell when she was angry, but when she came marching down the aisle and stopped by my desk with, "Hold out your hands and make fists," I knew she was really mad! She took a steel edged ruler out of the sleeve of her gown and hit me over the knuckles; whack, whack, whack! It hurt a little but I didn't let her know.

I was embarrassed and didn't want to face the other kids, so when school let out I ran home and waited for Mom.

When she came in the house I said, "I'm not going back to school ." "What do you mean?" "I'm just not." "Why?"

I told her the whole thing. She said, "You're not telling me the truth. You must've done something really bad for Sister to punish you, and you are going back to school" "No I'm not." "Yes you are." "No I'm not." "We'll see about that young man." We saw about it!

The next morning I took off my nightshirt and refused to dress. She dressed me.

I wouldn't walk toward school so she pulled a small branch from our lemon tree and switched my legs every time I stopped walking. We made it in record time, and Mom and Sister had a little conference they needn't have bothered with; because I already decided I wanted to stay in school so I could get smart enough to handle all the money I was going to make as a champion boxer.

Last night Dad and Rolly and I listened to the fight on the radio and heard that Jack Dempsey was getting $5,000 for just one fight. That was a lot of money.

The morning after we listened to the fight, Dad took Rolly and me and three buckets and three crow bars to the rocky area of Palos Verde beach.

We took home a full bucket of abalone and I got to "tenderize" them by pounding corn meal into them with a wooden tenderizing mallet.

I liked being a "provider".

The next day, Dad was in his soldier suit again because he was in "the reserves", but he soon quit wearing it because he was "mustered out". He kept on painting U.S.Navy ships with red lead and his coughing got worse and he had real bad hiccups. I thought he just had a bad cold but it never got better. I was six when the Dad I barely knew died. He "hiccuped" himself to death!

On a very hot day Mom and I, and my brother and two little sisters, rode in the back of a big black car, that followed another big black car about twenty five miles to Calvary Cemetery in East Los Angeles; where we buried Dad.

Mom cried a lot. I knew it was up to me to help. Happy kid times were over; I had to grow up fast.

It made me feel better when I visited my friend Newell Swan who lived on a farm just across the alley from Grandpa. He had asthma, so his folks bought him cigarettes called Cubeb, so he could breathe easier.

Newell and I would crawl up into the loft of their barn and sit cross-legged on the planks, watching and grinning at each other as we smoked.

This was better than the cigars and didn't make me choke.

Newell's sickness kept him from helping me with my war against the "messicuns"; some of whom later became my best friends and employees.

One of the enemy named Felix, shot at me with his Benjamin Pump BB gun. The shot came through a crack in the fence that I was looking through., and hit me just above my right eye. I lost the eyebrow for a little while, but luckily didn't lose the eye.

Felix bragged that he was the world's champion shooter, but later said he didn't even know I was looking through that crack. The shot was as lucky for him as it was for me.

When I took time out from my "war", and from smoking with Newell, I went to see the Sheehy kids, at their big dairy a couple of miles down a dirt road. I walked there almost every day to visit with the three boys while they did the milking.

As I walked through the milking shed the guys aimed the cow's teats at me and squirted me with milk.

I thought that to be great fun, but when I visited the cow barns at county fairs I found cows to be no fun at all.

Whenever I was looking at the cows on display they would plop their stuff on the ground right next to me, splashing my shoes and pant legs!

That helped me decide that I hated cows and anything that came from them, so it was good that I no longer needed milk.

God makes no mistakes, so I no longer needed anything from cows!

He brought me into the world with no teeth so I had to live off of mother's milk, then when I got a little older He gave me baby teeth so I ate only soft things like white bread, soft mush, and jellied cranberry sauce.

We went on living in Grandpa's house while Mom earned our food money working for a doctor in Nadeau. Aunt Bea and Uncle Frank lived next door and looked after us while Mom was gone. Mexican Annie kept us at her house when Aunt Bea was away.

Annie sure made good burritos!

Grandpa had lost his wife before I came and now he lost his only child. He was very lonely, so he turned to Mom for affection, which made Mom very uneasy; and made me even more angry with him.

The situation worsened, so we moved in with Mom's folks in Alhambra, California.

Mom drove back and forth to her job in Nadeau, which was about twenty miles away.

She was practical nurse and receptionist for Dr. Ward Sechrist.

Doctor Sechrist became our family doctor and took care of all of the "health needs", that a family of four kids had.

No longer living next door to Newell, I gave up smoking Cubebs.

I must've had a lot of will power, because this was the second time I gave up smoking and I was only seven.

When I was eight Mom enlisted me in the fourth grade at All Souls, just one block from our new home. Marengo Public School was just across the street from Grandma's.

There was a tall chain link fence between the two schools, where we spent our recess time yelling "pup lickers" at the public school kids in response to their "cat licker" taunts; like the Catholic-Protestant thing in Ireland, except we did't kill each other.

Mom and all four grandparents were Roman Catholic so there was no doubt which side of that fence I would be on. Grandpa Lodjic was Polish, Grandma Lodjic was Irish, Grandpa Sager was Swiss from the German sector, and Grandma Sager was French.

Each left their family in the "old country" and met their "spouse to be" when they entered the United States at Ellis Island. Loneliness brought them quickly together.

The immigration officer had no trouble understanding any of them except Grandpa Lodjic, whose ability with the English language was zilch, so Mladjewski ended up being Lodjic!

That eased the chore of signing my name. "Thank you Mr. Immigration Officer".

Whenever anyone, seeing my name for the first time, asked my nationality I replied, "I was named by an Immigration officer and I'm Heinz". Their slogan, "57 Varieties", seemed to fit.

While I was going to All Souls school, my principal interests were communication, travel, and construction. Reader's Digest and Time were my favored passtimes.

I wanted to be involved, but at that age I could do no more than read and re-read the happenings such as Lindberg's flight from New York to Paris, and the exceptional feat of construction of Hoover Dam.

Mr. Hoover, our new president, was himself a brilliant engineer. To honor him Congress named the marvelous dam, between Nevada and Arizona, Hoover Dam. I was fascinated by Reader's Digest's story telling of this "engineering marvel" on which the final cost was much below the estimate for the first and only time in public works history.

Hoover Dam created the world's largest man-made lake, called Lake Mead, at Boulder City, Nevada.

During the few years that Mom continued working for Dr. Sechrist in Nadeau, she went regularly to dances there, that were sponsored by a Christian group called "Maccabees"; who took their name from the son of an ancient Jewish priest, Judas Maccabeus. It was at one of those dances that Mom met the guy who would be my new dad. I was ten when I first saw him. I thought he had a very big face because he had no hair and I couldn't tell where his face ended, but I liked him from the start and was certain that Mom brought him home to get my OK.

My brother didn't pay him much attention and my sisters were scared of him; but because I approved, they married and I got to be best man!

I was eleven when Sumpter Roy Straley and Wilhelmina Josephina Sager (Lodjic) were married in the front room of Grandma's two story house in Alhambra, California.

Father Mark of All Souls Catholic Church did the knotting at Grandma's because he couldn't marry them in the church unless Dad became a Catholic.

Grandpa Lodjic continued to live in his house in Nadeau next to his brother Frank in an area that was a part of Watts; where very destructive rioting took place because people of color weren't being treated right. Grandpa was ninety-five when cancer took him. I didn't go to his funeral.

My big strong new dad was called "Sump" by his friends, but he let us kids call him Dad because we were special. He drove a big truck for a Los Angeles carpet and linoleum company. He told me he needed a swamper. "What's that?"
"Swamper is what they call a truck drivers helper."

Once when I was "swamping" I needed to go to the bathroom, but in '28 there were no rest stops, and service stations were few and far between; so we had to find a place where I could hide behind bushes or trees. There weren't many of those either.
Dad saw me squirming and handed me his big felt hat, "Here use this". I laughed nervously and forgot my urgency until he found a place where there were trees and undergrowth. I survived, but barely.

While we lived with Grandpa and Grandma Sager, Rolly and I fought constantly. He would give me a provoking poke and I would chase him around and around the house with the ax that I grabbed when we first passed the tool storage corner. I don't think I would have split his head, but I wanted him to think I would.
Dad decided to do something about it. He grabbed us each by a shoulder and fast-trotted us out to the garage where he locked us in to fight it out. "When it's quiet because only one of you is still alive I'll come let that one out".

We sparred around a bit until we suddenly realized one of us was supposed to die. "Let us out we're done!"

Dad let us sweat it for a while, then opened the door with a surprised look. "You're both still alive!", then warned; "There better be no "next time" or you'll be left there until neither is alive." We gave it up.

One day I got mad at Mom and Dad and said, "I'm not goin' to live here anymore". Dad said, "OK, take off all of your clothes." "Why?"

"You came that way, so you leave that way." I changed my mind.

For a guy who left school when he finished the fourth grade, to work the farm with his dad, he sure was savvy.

Grandpa Sager was a piano and violin teacher and tuner and insisted I become a concert violinist. I hated every moment of it and practiced too many hours every day; hours I could have used climbing trees.

Grandpa kept his appointments on his bicycle, but his business grew to the point he felt he needed more convenient transportation. He went to the local Chevy dealer and paid four-hundred dollars for a new sedan. After no more than a demo-ride, accompanied by the salesman, he drove it home. The short drive unnerved him so much he had Dad put the car up on blocks in the garage where it stayed as long as he was alive. It took up the space where Rolly and I would fight it out to the death if ever we got out of line again, but Grandpa's insistence I learn to play the violin left no time for fighting.

When Grandpa got his new car, I expected to get his bicycle for my two hundred customer paper route, but since he wouldn't drive it, that never happened; so I continued taking it on roller skates.

I wore out four pair, and got strong legs for running, which I enjoyed second only to apeing like Tarzan. Swinging limb to limb and tree to tree, through the big pepper trees that ringed the grounds of Marengo school, I traversed the entire city block.

I was seven when Mom had me operated on to take out my tonsils and adenoids; without telling me that she also arranged for me to be circumcised.

I was concerned that I hurt between my legs from having my tonsils out. The nurse thought that to be very funny, but I didn't.

Fielding Hayes and I were co-leaders of our Marengo gang, because we were the best fighters. The other guys were Frenchy and Carl and Eugene Eckhart.

We didn't smoke or drink or terrorize anybody, we just played football and baseball together, and spent a lot of time "skinny dipping" in a pond that was in an abandoned rock quarry on the outskirts of town.

We would dive off the rocks, swim to the side and then climb back up to the diving spot.

As we sat in the sun to dry off, the guys were pointing at me and laughing. "What's funny?" "You got a weird dingy". I was the only one that had been circumcised!

I wouldn't have chosen that way of being set apart from the crowd, but I could live with it.

The entire time we lived with Grandpa and Grandma I served as an altar boy at All Souls, and was the only male voice in the choir. One of the Sisters played the organ and two of them sang along with two old ladies who were probably twenty or twenty-five. Some of the songs were in Latin so I didn't know what we were saying, but learned to make the right sounds.

I was a good Catholic, so I went to confession every Saturday and took Communion every Sunday. Early mass at six o'clock was always crowded because you couldn't eat or drink before you had Communion, which had to follow right after confession for the forgiveness to work.

Since that made me "ready to die", I always ran home to get breakfast, because I didn't want to die hungry.

I also didn't want sins on my record and have to suffer through purgatory, so I said the number of "Our Fathers" and "Hail Marys" that the priest in the little box told me to say. I told him the same things every week, but he didn't seem to notice; and I didn't notice if the penance was always the same.

Being Catholic was easy, all I had to do was to memorize the prayers and say them the right number of times and Father Mark forgave me of my sins. I supposed if I did something really bad I'd have to go to Rome and have the Pope forgive me.

I thought maybe I should ask Father Mark, "Would I need a letter of introduction or could I just knock on the Pope's door?" I sure wouldn't want to go all that way and have him refuse to see me!

I knew all about Jesus: he was a baby born in Bethlehem and his mother's name was Virgin Mary, and when he grew up some bad people put him on a cross where he died.

I knew what He and his Mom looked like because we had big statues of them in our church and we had to genuflect every time we walked in front of them.

I left All Souls and finished grammar school with my eighth grade at Marengo where I changed sides and joined in calling the kids across the fence "cat-lickers". Those Irish people should change sides and quit killing each other.

Dad's family was Methodist, so we quit going to the Catholic church and I switched to the public school where we didn't have to pay. I started high school at Alhambra High when I was twelve.

There was no such thing as pre-school or middle school; you had eight years of grammar school and four years of high school, and that was it. If you graduated, and had a little money, you went to junior college; and if you had lots of money you got to go to a university.

While we were living with Grandma, the French family in the house behind her moved away. I thought they owned the place, but when I met the owner and went to work for him, I found they didn't.

But while they still lived there I noticed the older girl, Yvonne, was always leaving with different guys in big fancy cars. I guessed it was because she was so pretty that she had so many rich boyfriends, but when they moved I said something to Mom about it and she told me what was really going on and that it was, "Yvonne's business, not mine!"

The owner asked me if I would help him tear the place down so he could build apartments. He would pay me twenty-five cents an hour. I went to work.

These were Depression years and Mom and Dad needed all the help they could get.

After we removed the shingles and tar felt we began to tear down the roof framing. I was up on the framing and needed to go to the bathroom.

I jumped down and one "tennis shoed" foot landed on a shingle with rusty nails sticking up. One nail went through the sole and through my foot, about an inch behind my toes. I stepped on the shingle with the other foot and pulled my impaled one loose. As I started to climb back up on the roof there was a loud roaring in my head. I swooned and passed out.

Mom was mopping the screened porch on the rear of Grandma's house, and she saw me drop.

She plunged the mop into the bucket, then came charging out and sloshed it on my face.

It worked. I came to and went back to work.

I couldn't have said I was no worse for the wear and tear and the dirty mop water in my face, but I was tough as those nails and ignored it. Anyway, there was no such thing as sick pay in '29, so I couldn't afford time off.

The next day I helped my boss finish the job and got my five dollar severance pay for those last two ten hour days. When I went into the house Mom checked further on the reason for my having passed out. She found a purple streak going from my foot up into my groin and hurried me to the doctor.

He was able to take care of it without my going to the hospital.

The French family and the limousines would never return and I would miss Yvonne's constant coming and going.

One day, when I finished my paper route, I was riding fast as I could down a long hill near home. The front tire blew and fouled in the forks, throwing my groin into the frame and the handlebars, causing a rupture. Painfully, I picked up my bike and carried it home.

For several days I kept secret that I had a big lump in my right groin, but my brother saw it and told Mom. Back to the hospital I went for a hernia operation.

A few weeks later I went with the Boy Scouts to a sulphurous lake called Elsinore down near San Diego. It was too hot to not be in or on the water so I spent about five hours in a rented kayak.

I was fiery red over all my body except the small amount covered by my swim suit, so I learned, "Guys with blond curly hair and a freckled face should cover up".

At the end of a miserable two-hour trip, the scoutmaster let me out at the corner about a block from home. I started walking but was soon down on all fours. I crawled the last half block and barely made it up the front steps. Mom heard the thunk when I fell against the front screen door. She opened the door, dragged me in, filled the tub with cold water and dunked me. Back to the hospital I went, for treatment for sunstroke and for third degree burns over most of my body!

With all the money I was making from my paper route and the wrecking job, I might've been able to buy some stock and get rich enough to go to Stanford University, but the Lord was in charge and I didn't buy any.

If I had, I would have lost it all, because at the New York Stock Exchange on October 29, 1929 a record 16.410,030 shares were traded, as huge blocks of stocks were sold for whatever one could get. The total value of stocks dropped twenty six billion dollars! That was far more than the Federal budget.

The economy suffered world wide. There was no place to run or to hide.

The Great Depression was years of misery for many, but for me they were some of the happiest days of my childhood.

Costs were at an all time low and Mom and Dad wanted a place of their own. It was time for them to build their nest. With $200 down and a mortgage for $2000, Dad had a contractor friend build a three bedroom house to his and Mom's specifications; and I had fun and saved the folks money by doing all of the clean-up.

The new place was in another section of Alhambra so I got to stay at Alhambra High. I was thirteen when we moved.

The City Park was a block from home, so it took only a few minutes for me to get there. I got a job making hamburgers at the refreshment stand working 4:15pm until 8:00. My boss paid me twenty cents an hour and all the hamburgers and fries I could eat. I could also have all the pop I wanted. But since I didn't want to get fat I made sure the hamburger was well done and didn't eat fries or drink pop.

My boss saved the cost of the fries and pop, I saved myself the cost of getting to be a "blubber butt and gut", and Mom and Dad saved on the grocery bill. And, I was an entrepreneur again with two incomes.

On my fourteenth birthday Mom gave me my first and only birthday party. The party was mostly family except for a girl from up the street named Bonnie Baker, who later gained fame as a singing radio personality known as "Wee Bonnie Baker".

After the party, at about nine in the evening, I walked Bonnie home. We detoured to the park that was a half block away and sat on a bench and talked. I was gone a little more than an hour.

When I got home Mom opened the back door to let me in, picked up a piece of firewood from the bin by the door and hit me on the top of my head saying, "I know just what you've been doing and I want you to never do that again!"

I didn't know what Mom's problem was, but at that point in life mine was that I was afraid of girls.

But, there was no sense in arguing, so I shook off the mist and went to bed.

One of Dad's favorite sayings was, "If you want to get a mule's attention, hit him over the head with a two by four. I guess Mom thought I was "mule-like".

A few weeks later the folks took the rest of the kids to Los Angeles to shop. They would be gone several hours so I decided to make some wine. I squeezed a bunch of white seedless grapes and poured the juice into six pint bottles. I put a little yeast in each, and put caps on them, using the bottle capper I had used on Dad's beer bottles in Grandma's cellar. I opened the crawl hole under the house and crawled a long way in to hide them, and left them to age.

I forgot them until five or six months later when the folks and kids were gone again. Four of the six bottles were broken. I grabbed the other two, crawled out from under the house and took them into the kitchen.

I used the bottle opener on the first and it sprayed over the entire kitchen: floor, walls, ceiling, and appliances; so I opened the remaining one under a small pan with a large pan under it.

Voila!, I reaped the benefits of labor and patience. It was delicious.

Time ran out, the folks would soon return. I got the step stool, a bucket of soapy water, and some rags and scrubbed the entire kitchen and appliances. Just as I finished the cover-up I heard the car drive in. I grabbed my "Homer's Iliad" and was in my bedroom totally engrossed in the huge tome that was required reading for my English class.

The next day I got a job as helper to a milkman, who had the Arden Farms route in the wealthy section of Pasadena.

After a short time I found that he had a problem with another kind of bottle. He phoned me just after midnight, and said he was sick, so I would have to run the route alone.

Pasadena had an ordinance that all commercial delivery trucks had to be off the roads by five in the morning. I got up at two and went to the cold storage facility and loaded the truck.

I decided that I could save time if I put the truck in low gear and walked alongside it while loading the milk basket, and then catch up with it before the next stop.

It was a great time saving idea, but as I was walking alongside the slow moving truck, loading the basket, the rear wheels rolled over both of my feet. I painfully completed the route and gave up my "brainstorm".

When I was a high school junior, at six-foot-one, weighing a hundred and fifty pounds, I played quarterback position on the "B" team. I wasn't heavy enough for the Varsity squad.

We played sixty minutes in whatever position we had. There was no such thing as "offense" and "defense".

After some of the games I went home with one or more fingernails hanging by a thread. They were torn out when I tackled.

Dad would say, "Let me see that", and take the loose nail between his thumb and forefinger and jerk it loose. After a few such treatments I pulled them off while I showered in the locker room.

It didn't occur to either of us to use a scissors.

The two seasons that I quarterbacked, we never lost a game. We even won a scrimmage with our varsity; but to them it was just practice, to us it was a challenge.

I was also on the wrestling team and gymnastic team. I could do the rope climb faster than anyone in school except Melvin. He had withered legs and would grab the rope, and pull himself up out of his wheelchair, like a spider on a web.

He made me aware that handicaps can be overcome and even used to advantage!

Everything seemed to be going well but a sad time was on the way. Grandpa Sager's habit was to come home about five o'clock, put his bicycle in the garage, take off his coat and bow-tie and go into the bathroom and wash up.

The routine was always exactly the same; he put on a sweater, went out the front door, got in the rocking chair under the huge pepper tree in the front yard and immediately fell asleep.

Grandma would go out and touch him on the shoulder with, "Time to eat Pa."

On a fateful day in '31 she touched him and shook him gently but he couldn't wake up.

He was sleeping with the saints. He left Planet Earth serenely in his sleep. What a way to go!

He was a gentle being to whom the Lord gave a life of serenity without sickness or disability. He obeyed God's commandments and knew the Lord so he's now enjoying eternal bliss in the mansion reserved for him; and he's probably alternating playing piano and violin for the heavenly choir.

We'll hear him and the choir when we get there, but I don't think I'll ask for more lessons.

Grandma was now alone and needed family around so Mom and Dad sold the new house and we moved back in with her.

With no more mortgage payments on the new house, and with the rental income from Grandma's duplex and cottage, along with Dad's occasional paycheck and my pay from the paper route, milk route, and hamburger stand; we had more than enough to get by.

"Helping to get by" seemed to be my assignment.

Grandma couldn't survive the loneliness of the loss of her husband of sixty years, and the added loss of her only son. Uncle Joe had been in the Marine Corps in China for several years, and would have been Mom's joint heir to Grandma's estate, but died from a self-inflicted bullet wound to the head following his retirement from The Corps and a surprising marriage.

When Grandma died, Mom called the junkman; who was a white-whiskered elderly jewish man. He came with his horse and buggy and hauled away Grandpa's upright grand piano. Grandpa had brought it over from Switzerland. It was solid black ebony and had silver candlestick holders on the upright face.

Mom needed the space and the fifty dollars!

I had lost my dad and my grandfather, now I lost my only uncle and the only grandmother that I knew; and I never had an aunt.

Mom and Dad and my brother and two sisters were my entire family, but it didn't occur to me that my situation was different, except when my buddies talked about their fun at family picnics.

But who knows, I might have kin in Ireland, Poland, France or Switzerland, if ever I'm curious enough to find out.

With the properties to look after and a family to take care of, Mom no longer worked away from home; and with the depression at full depth and Dad with no job, income from the rentals and what I brought in was insufficient.

Dad went to work in Franklin Roosevelt's SERA program repairing trails in the San Dimas canyon above Monrovia, California. He had a dentist friend who happened to have a cabin there, so we moved out of Grandma's big house and rented it out.

In spite of the bad times, we had a good times mountain cabin vacation. The cabin had two bedrooms. Mom and Dad used the smaller one and we four kids slept on cots in the other. The toilet, two hundred feet behind the cabin, was a little hut with a new moon carved in the door. We learned about recycling the Sears and Roebuck catalog.

The bath, only fifty feet behind the cabin, was another little hut. It had a "draw curtain" and had a half-gallon tomato can with holes in it hanging from the ceiling; so we also learned about cold water bathing!

A pail of water was pulled out of the cistern and poured into the bucket with holes in the bottom. We got under the shower and soaped, then poured another bucketful into the can to rinse.

It was fun except in real cold weather.

When drawing up the water bucket, we had to be careful to not scoop up the salamanders. They kept "stuff" out of our drinking water.

SERA paid the workers in scrip that could be used to buy food at the Central Market in Los Angeles.

It wouldn't buy alcohol or cigarettes; that was certainly a good way to handle welfare.

Canned Spam was the only meat the scrip would buy so we had a steady diet of it.

It's amazing what one can accept out of necessity. Normally I couldn't stand the looks of Spam, let alone the smell. The addicts probably traded their's for cigarettes.

Fortunately the SERA program soon ended, so we moved back into Grandma's house and never "Spam'd" again!

Mom and Dad sold the rental units and purchased a service station in Alhambra at the corner of Valley Boulevard and Marengo Street. There was a service station on each corner.

We soon found ourselves in a price war. Every time one station dropped its price a fraction the other three dropped theirs a little more. We were gifting a gallon with each gallon purchased. The price was five cents a gallon.

In spite of the low overhead; because Rolly and I pumped gas, washed windshields, greased cars and repaired tires without pay; we weren't making enough to survive.

One of our regular customers who always drove big expensive cars suggested that Dad could make good money acting as the go-between with his customers. Dad was to hand the addressed package to the customer and take the cash for Mr. Big, who would give Dad twenty percent of the amount collected. We ate regularly again but the deal was short lived because Prohibition was repealed just a few weeks after the arrangement.

Dad took Rolly and me to the brewery in L.A. where they piped the drinking fountains with the "near" beer in order to quickly start brewing the full strength stuff. We drank to our capacity and enjoyed the peanuts and pickled eggs that were free with the drinking fountain beer.

The economy improved and Dad went back to work for his former employer as an installer of carpet and linoleum. Mom too was newly busy; she was again with child.

Larry was Mom and Dad's only progeny, and was a healthy and happy addition.

Dad's mom and dad and four sisters and three brothers were now a part of our family, but none had children so we became kids of the whole group; and Larry as their only nephew got lots of attention. Dad's family's joys and trials and those of our family seemed to merge. There was always much to talk about.

One of Dad's sisters, Fay, was a Methodist missionary and didn't approve of the "wine and beer making" in the cellar nor the card playing in the sitting room. Although disapproval showed on her face, she was diplomatic and never voiced it, so it never dampened our joyful spirits.

At fifteen I was number two man in the family because Roland joined the Navy to have fun, and to relieve our cost of living. One day he was home on leave and sitting on the fender of my '21 Ford roadster, parked in the driveway behind the house. I was looking out the upstairs window and saw Frenchy, the kid who used to live in the old house behind us, walk up to Rolly and hit him heavily on the jaw. Not expecting it, Rolly just shook his head and looked stunned. Frenchy had figured that Rolly was trying to take away his girlfriend.

I ran down the street in the direction he had gone and found him in the house of some friends. I went inside, grabbed him around the middle and carried him out to the front lawn. As I wrestled him onto the grass, and was beating his face with my fists, my blonde curly-head little sister, Bernice, began tugging on me; "Carl let him up, stop it you're going to kill him. Stop it!" When he seemed completely done in I got off him and went home.

Perhaps my ferocity came from a desire to get even: In a sandlot ball game Frenchy was at bat and I was catching. He swung at the ball, purposely making a full revolution, and hit me full force on the side of my head as I rose to catch it.

However, I held no grudge against him for either incident as we had been friends a long time and had street-fought with common enemies.

But, despite having fought often with my brother, I wasn't about to let anyone take advantage of him.

A week later, Frenchy was among the group when I took my gang down to Hermosa Beach and was driving back up to Alhambra on Atlantic Boulevard. We smelled smoke and saw it coming out of the turtleback. I pulled off the road, opened the lid and saw that the car was on fire. We had thrown our swim shorts and towels in the back and a loose tire tool fell across the battery poles igniting the cloth.

It was such a hot blaze we could do nothing to quench it. We stood and watched for a short time but, fearing an explosion, I got the guys to help me tip it over into the wet ditch alongside the road.

We grabbed the fenders and running board and rolled it over. We put up our thumbs and hitched a ride home.

I never went back to see what happened to the wreckage, but got up early to see if there was anything in the newspaper about a burnt and abandoned car. No mention was made.

Roland was still in the Navy when I graduated from high school in '33; and enrolled in the School of Journalism at Los Angeles Junior College, the original campus of UCLA.

Mom and Dad had decided that if they were going to help any of us go on to higher learning it would be me.

I studied to become a newspaper reporter. I ran the advertising department for the school paper and was paid a small amount every month through a federal aid program; without which we couldn't have afforded my extra education.

I hadn't previously known any Jewish kids but had heard lots of bad jokes about "jews".

My best friend at L.A.J.C. was a long and lanky guy named Jerry Lubovisky who became a vice-president of Union Oil Company. Jerry's uncle, Carmen Lubovisky, was a renowned concert violinist. Grandpa would beam with delight knowing that Carmen gave a private concert for Jerry and me, in his home, while I danced with Carmen's daughter.

My Etymology professor, Isadore Colodny, was also Jewish. He gave me a good understanding of the derivation and composition of words.

I have never had racial prejudice; I am only what I was born to be, so I see nothing special in being gentile and colorless.

In my job as Ad manager for the school paper, I was soliciting advertising from the Los Angeles Philharmonic Orchestra. Its principal backer was a lady named Leland Atherton Irish.

Mrs. Irish agreed to purchase space in our school paper if I agreed to be volunteer Publicity and Public Relations manager for the Orchestra.

This was my first experience in volunteerism and paved the way for my continuing interest in such activity. Other benefits included free admission to the Symphony rehearsals and performances, and a good appreciation for this finer art.

Mom and Dad sold all the Alhambra properties and bought a home on Mentor Street in the northeast section of Pasadena. One day my car wouldn't start so I rode the bus from Pasadena to school.

When school was out I realized I didn't have money to pay bus fare home.

I started walking and put up my thumb. Soon a fancy car stopped and the door opened. A nicely dressed guy asked where I wanted to go. I told him I was going home to north Mentor Street in Pasadena. Starting to drive, he put his hand over on my upper leg with a silly grin on his face, and said, "That's just where I'm going!" I cocked my fist and said, "Pull over and stop the car or your closest relative will never recognize you."

He looked at my face and knew I meant it. He pulled over and waited for me to get out, then sped down the street as though the devil he served was on his tail! I thumbed another ride.

When I was eighteen I joined the National Guard. I went for drill practice every Wednesday evening and on field maneuvers two times a year. After I had attained the rank of Sergeant, the Guard was called out to maintain law and order at the docks in San Francisco; when non-union help had to be used because the Longshoremen went on strike, threatening the sustenance of the people.

My squad had a machine gun nest atop a flatiron shaped building, at the entrance to the docks.

I posted one man to stop and to check all vehicles attempting entry and another to query and divert pedestrians. I had instructed my men not to fire until ordered, and when ordered, to fire only into the air unless force was displayed. When a truck tried to enter the area by refusing to stop at the sentry post I ordered them to fire.

The burst of gunfire brought the truck to an abrupt stop and a badly shaken driver spun around and sped away.

In '35 when I graduated from the School of Journalism, I asked the Placement office for a list of openings in either journalism or advertising.

If neither was available I wanted a listing of companies needing a typist. Hemphill Diesel Schools was the only listing and they needed a typist. I applied and went to work as soon as I filled out the application. I was now the forty dollar a month typist of Hemphill's Los Angeles office. The backlog of work was immense; I worked fourteen hours a day six days a week.

When the typing was no longer backlogged the manager asked if I would like to be Chief Clerk, since that position had just been vacated. I jumped at the chance for this unanticipated promotion. Now I was Chief Clerk as well as "the" typist. I asked the manager if I was to have a raise. He said, "We are most pleased with your work but unable at this moment to afford it." A few weeks later I was asked if I wanted to be Purchasing Agent. Gullible as I was, I also jumped at that chance.

Now I was Purchasing Agent and Chief Clerk, and still "the" typist.

Again I asked about a raise and again was told they were pleased but financially unable.

The least they could have done was to give me some fancy new title!

I asked the manager if when I was caught up with my work I could take the time off. He so readily agreed that I'm certain he didn't want me to quit, and didn't want to give me his job to keep me.

I did some job seeking by calling on the City Editor of The Los Angeles Illustrated Daily News, a tabloid newspaper of good reputation. Matt Weinstein told me they could use me, and my salary would be forty dollars a month. I asked what it took to rise over the forty dollar figure. He said that when I was no longer a cub, through having by-line stories, I would receive a raise. "How long does that usually take?" "I have six cubs on the payroll, and some have been here for two years."

Oh well, bye-bye Journalism. I didn't have time to climb that ladder.

Whenever Mom found some kid who she thought needed a home she brought him to our home, and when I got there late at night I'd find him in my big bed with perhaps others she had taken in.

Life was interesting with a Mom who couldn't resist "kids in need".

One such was a tall, gangly kid named Art who was the brother of the son-in-law of the president and principal owner of a large steel fabricating company in Los Angeles. I asked if they had any openings. He would check and let me know the next day.

Art found that they needed a shop-billing clerk and arranged an interview with the General Superintendent of Pacific Iron and Steel Co., Ltd., near Lynwood, California. I was to be there at 7:30 the next morning. I arrived at 7:00. This impressed Mr. John Bertone, so being early continued to be my habit.

I wanted also to impress him with my neatness, so I made certain my hair was cut short, the only way a real man would ever have it. Also I dressed in my best and only suit, a wide flowered tie, shiny black shoes, and a long overcoat.

Looking back I realized that my attire looked like that of a comic book character in a Zoot suit, but I got the job and started work the next morning.

I didn't feel inclined to give Hemphill notice. The manager could have the two days pay and could handle the job until he found someone else to take advantage of the wonderful opportunity of all those promotions!

May 9, 1936, my nineteenth birthday, was a real milestone in my life. On that day I traded my typing job for the job of shop billing clerk. I was to make a "take off" of materials from the detail drawings; creating "cutting lists" to give the cutting machine operators the needed information for cutting to size and shape every piece of steel that would be fabricated into components of a particular structure.

The components would be put together in the field on the customer's foundation, to frame a building, an industrial structure, or a tank.

For a nineteen-year-old, who had claimed to be twenty-one to be sure he was hired; and had never even heard the term "steel fabricating", this was a challenge.

I gathered every old drawing I could find and studied them all night long. The next morning with only an occasional question for the cutting yard foreman, I tackled the backlog of "cutting lists".

That backlog and updating of inventory files kept me working from seven in the morning until midnight every day for months.

I was putting in seventeen hours a day plus a half hour driving each way seven days a week, but I was now being paid sixty dollars a month instead of the forty dollars of my previous jobs.

With my three-hundred-and-ninety-hour months this figured to be a little over fifteen cents an hour, but the sixty-dollar a month figure was the important thing.

Also, it was enticing to have the opportunity to learn all the trades of the business.

I went after that learning like a starved puppy.

At times I was used as a helper on one or another of the cutting machines or punches or drills. I then learned how to properly use a cutting torch and a welding machine. Next I learned the more technical functions of layout, fitting, and checking.

I completed score one of my life and began my odyssey to create something to benefit mankind.

Score 2

"Climbing years".
(Climbing the corporate ladder, from lowest paid flunky to
President and principal owner.)

About the end of my first year at Pacific Iron & Steel Co., Ltd., I called the main office to talk with the Chief Estimator. A new voice answered. We had a new receptionist and telephone operator. I liked the voice and introduced myself. She sounded interested but guarded.

After querying Art Simpson about her I asked her for a date. Art worked in the head office in Highland Park, and had also asked for a date. She had put him off, as she did me, but my persistence paid off with a "yes" after a few weeks of trying.

We had a hamburger with everything on it, and went to the movies; total cost: fifty cents!

After the third date I asked her to marry me. She said she would have to think about it. To my response of, "If you don't know now you probably never will!" she said, "I'll let you know in about a week."

I've never been known for my patience.

The second date after my proposal Mary said she would marry me if I would go to church with her. I went with her to the Methodist Church, in Compton, California. After which I told her, "I could never enjoy a church where the pastor gives "hellfire and brimstone" messages such as we just heard."

We agreed we would together find the church that felt right for both of us.

We planned the marriage for June 6.

I wanted a better car to drive my "bride-to-be" to our wedding and to our honeymoon cottage; so for our vacations, Art Simpson and I were going to drive my '23 Chrysler roadster to Pontiac, Michigan to buy new (second owner) cars and drive them home.

One of Mom's stray kids was in the Navy and was about to hitch hike to his folk's home in Iowa.

Mom hinted that I might give him a ride, so he and our luggage sat in the rumble seat. We had agreed to take him as close to his home as our chosen route provided.

Freeways and cross-country highways were not in existence, so I was driving on a dirt road near Leadville, Colorado when we blew a rear tire.

The car went out of control. I steered for a ten-foot embankment on the uphill side to avoid a very deep chasm on the other!

The car turned over backward. Art and I had only a few bruises but the sailor had one side of his face peeled back from chin to forehead by the rain gutter around the rumble seat.

Fortunately, there was a hospital in the area because of a huge construction project to take water from the Colorado River to Los Angeles.

The sailor was operated on, and was told that he would be in the hospital for three days. We stayed until he was released and the three of us hitched a ride into town where we went on by Greyhound bus.

My Chrysler roadster was wiped out and resided in the local junkyard.

I had now owned two cars and both were demolished!

In Pontiac, Michigan I bought a '34 Hudson and Art bought a '31 Ford. We drove back to Pasadena together, so that if either had a problem the other could help; and made it home trouble-free.

On June 6, 1938 Mary Frances Charles became Mary Frances Lodjic in the Santa Barbara County courthouse.

Although I was eager for the marriage I would not accede to having to get parental consent, so we waited thirty-three days beyond my 21st birthday.

I wanted to know that I alone was in total human control of my life.

Mary wouldn't be twenty-one until October 27, but the law permitted a girl to marry without consent, after she became eighteen.

Judge Bigler officiated in a ritual that took ten minutes, but lasted fifty-two years.

We ran down the stairs and got in our car to return to our little rented cottage in Compton.

As we started to drive off I became aware that I wasn't as "in control" of my life as I had intended.

I had forgotten to pay the judge.

I ran up the two flights of stairs, knocked on his office door and gave him a twenty-dollar bill. "Thanks, sorry I forgot."

That twenty dollars wouldn't qualify me as, "One of the last of the big spenders," but it represented one hundred and thirty four hours of work.

We weren't allowed time off for a honeymoon, but we couldn't have afforded one anyway.

To celebrate, we shopped at a roadside market on the way home and bought a mop and a broom; no big bash with thousands of dollars squandered.

The Pacific Iron main office was soon moved to the location of the plant, so Mary and I could've rode together; but because of my erratic time schedule we usually drove separately.

I had just been given a raise to eighty dollars a month and our families had joined together for a party at which we were presented with discarded furniture and a couple of boxes of canned foods. It was the only time that our two families got together.

With our thirty-dollar a month rent and our car payment and utility costs we had enough left over for a weekly date of a hamburger and movie!

We felt like millionaires, and always paid our bills the day we got them so they wouldn't worry us.

No credit cards, we believed in paying cash or waiting until we could.

Mary quit the Methodist church because I refused to go where they preached, "If you have a falling out with God you can get back in with Him through doing good things."

We both knew that the only way to be in God's good favor was through knowing His son Jesus, and that there was and is no other way to the better life.

It was suggested by a friend of Mary's that the Episcopal church might be a good compromise; but we found it to be a watering down of the Catholic dependence on a human intercessor, mingled with the Methodist belief that you could make the grade with good works. We continued to look.

About a month after we married, President Roosevelt signed a document raising the minimum hourly wage from twenty-five cents to forty cents, except for farm workers, but I was on a salary so the president's order brought no additional money.

Just before our marriage the stock market recession bottomed out and relief rolls showed one million fewer participants than the year before, which made the future appear rosy; but many listed as "employed" were on tax-payer-supported work programs!

We were fortunate to both have jobs.

I completed my four-year hitch in the National Guard and was offered the commission of second lieutenant if I re-enlisted; but now I was married and had a child on "stork flight", so I didn't need the weekly eighty-mile round trip to Monrovia.

On September 1, 1939 Adolph Hitler's Nazi Germany invaded Poland, my grandfather's homeland.

A madman was beginning his quest to control the world and to annihilate everyone non-Aryan: more specifically, anyone who wasn't a disciple of his doctrine.

Great Britain and France declared war on Germany and President Franklin Roosevelt declared the U.S. as neutral, but we soon became part of the Allies.

This was the 2nd World War in my life. Dad was deferred in the first; and I was now deferred because my job as foreman of the graveyard shift made me valuable to the war effort.

My crew consisted of a few skilled men from the day shift, and a large number of "ladies of the night" working as moonlighters.

They were strong ambitious gals who challenged the men to strange contests during coffee break, but as long as they didn't peddle their wares during work hours and worked well, I was glad to have them and appreciated their patriotism.

Construction unrelated to the war effort was not permitted, so all our efforts were for the military or for war goods producers.

After the war ended, and I had held all shop positions, I was made foreman for the erection of the structural steel for a building for the Santa Barbara County Museum.

All civilian construction projects that had been put on hold were suddenly re-activated. Construction activity was so strong that personnel and rental equipment were extremely hard to find, so the only help I could get in Santa Barbara was that of the union business agent.

With a rented boom truck, because no mobile crane was available, he and I erected the three hundred tons in six working days.

I started erection work as a foreman so I never had a union card, but always worked alongside my crew, including the business agent, without difficulty.

My next field job was the erection of a 145' high by 300' long curved structure for Columbia Studios.

It was to be sheeted over with plywood, and would have scenery painted on it simulating the scenery of any place in the world. They would no longer have the delay or cost of transporting their acting crews and equipment to far off locations.

Their only cost for background scenery would be painting out the old and painting in the new.

Even the "spendthrift" entertainment business had to economize.

After I dismissed my ironworkers I was making a last minute check-up to be certain the job was properly completed.

As I walked across the 2"wide top member a strange looking new military aircraft went roaring by.

It was the first P38 out of the Lockheed barn in Burbank.

With its double fuselage and exceptional speed it fascinated me to the extent that I forgot where I was, until it was out of sight.

With the sudden realization that I was standing on a 2" wide piece of steel 145' in the air, I dropped down and wrapped my arms and legs tightly around it until the fright left.

I got up cautiously and completed the inspection.

Next, I was assigned to work under the supervision of the company's senior field foreman, Bill Windsor. The gang called him Wild Bill. If he disliked you he would fire you without comment.

His orders were law and he wouldn't tolerate anyone who, in his estimation, couldn't take it.

With one strike against me, because John Bertone had ordered him to put me in his crew, Wild Bill might fabricate an excuse to get rid of me.

I picked up the end of a twenty foot long 4" x 3"x 3/8"angle iron, not knowing that the other end was wedged under the steel plate casing we had just installed on a furnace at the Federal Prison on Terminal Island; offshore from Long Beach, California.

It snapped back down onto my right foot, smashing my big toe and two others. Wild Bill would've fired me, had I mentioned it, so I went on working with my foot sloshing around in the blood that gathered in my shoe.

The toe squashing happened just before lunch break. As I walked over to sit with the rest of the crew, one of our old hands, Leo Johnson, who went through a 6-pack of warm beer daily, saw me limping and asked about my foot. I told him what happened and asked if he would drive me home at quitting time. We left my car on the job-site and Leo "wavered" me home, up the highway.

Mary took me to the company doctor: a six-foot tall, two-hundred pound., physician who cut off my shoe and drilled holes in the toenails to relieve the blood pressure. As he drilled through the big toenail he had to put extra pressure on the drill and went through my toe and into his table.

Mary felt faint but I survived. Leo picked me up the next morning and took me back to the jobsite.

Many times I went home with eyes burned so badly, from welders arc, that Mary led me around like a puppy while I held a raw potato poultice on my eyes to draw out the pain.

The steel fabricating business was no place for the faint of heart.

When I was erecting hangar buildings for the Air Force or for the air-lines we often worked in areas right next to where the aircraft would start up, and warm up, their engines.

We wore no ear protectors because it lessened our ability to sense danger; but the aircraft noises, and those of pounding with a sixteen pound sledge-hammer while inside a tank; damaged my hearing.

However, I count as a blessing the lean body that came from the work effort.

No "blubber butt and gut" in this family!

I may never have had the opportunities for advancement if I had been hampered by the rulings of the Office of Safety and Health Administration, commonly known as OSHA. OSHA rulings, that came into effect soon after I had completed my shop and field training, would have hampered my "priority one", of getting the job done as well and as quickly as possible.

Leading my crew by setting a fast pace and outworking them, pleased my boss so much that I was regularly advanced through the various jobs within the company.

After being promoted to General Shop Foreman I was made Assistant Superintendent, then Field Superintendent and then General Superintendent; replacing the man who hired me, and from whom I had learned much of what I knew about the producing part of the business.

I wasn't winning a popularity contest with other employees; and "Wild Bill" quit in protest!

Company policy didn't allow pregnant women to work beyond the sixth month. Mary quit working the last day of March 1939.

Mary and I had agreed "early on" that most of the world's ills stemmed from overpopulation, and felt that Planet Earth was simply not meant to provide the necessities of life to so many; so we would have only two children, one to replace each of us.

In '39, when Michael was born, our country-type doctor warned, "From the shape of his head I can tell he will be a most difficult child." Mary and I merely smiled at the comment. We didn't believe in such foretelling, but became quickly aware that Michael was, and would continue to be, mischievous.

Our major immediate problem was that he often awoke during the night and bawled mightily. Our landlord asked us to move because other apartment tenants complained; so we had Dad's contractor friend construct, in Compton, California; a two-bedroom-and-den house of good solid construction.

It cost $3500 on a tax delinquency lot that we purchased through Bank of America for $150.

Corner lots were $300, but we felt we shouldn't go that much more in debt just to be on a corner.

I was still working long hours; so to assure my much-needed sleep Mary put Michael's crib in the other bedroom just down the hall. When he cried in the night she would get up and tend to his need without waking me.

One night, when she got up to quiet him, one of her legs was "asleep" and she turned her ankle and fell in the hall. I heard her fall and got up without turning on the light. Stumbling down the hall I kicked her in the face with my bare foot.

I turned on the light, grabbed her under both arms and dragged her to bed. She said, "This is not the way they do it in the movies!" I asked, "Is there anything I can do for you?" "Get me a glass of cold water from the icebox."

I got the glass of water, suddenly felt sick, and fainted as I was putting the pitcher back in the icebox.

When I fell, with the pitcher in hand, I scraped the back of my head on the two screws protruding from a cupboard door, where my head had broken off the handle. I got up, picked up the glass of water and went in the bedroom with blood running down the back of my pajamas.

I handed her the glass. She didn't say, "Thank you!"

She did say, "You get right back in this bed and don't move until I get back. I'm going down to Jo's and telephone for a doctor."

We couldn't afford a telephone and our nearest neighbor was about a half block away. Mary put on a robe, hobbled down the street on her sore ankle, and rang the doorbell at Jo's house. When she got no response she yelled, "Jo, I need to use your phone, Carl's hurt!"

When the operator answered she said, "I need a doctor!" The operator connected her with the Police Department.

They took the necessary information, rang the doctor on call, and sent two officers to the house.

When they rang the doorbell I let the two policemen in.

The first thing they saw was my bloodied pajamas and the blood-soaked towel on my head.

With water, broken glass, and blood on the kitchen floor and a trail of blood from the kitchen through the dining room and living room to a blood-soaked pillow on our bed; the place looked like a disaster area. Mary's swollen ankle and lip added to their impression.

While one policeman looked over the entire house, the other one said, "The doctor's on his way. While we wait for him we have to get the facts for the record." While the other policeman looked over the entire house, we gave him an exact account.

When writing it in his record book he mumbled, "I don't believe any of this. You had a fight and don't want to admit it." The other policeman nodded consent.

That might have been the case with his usual customers but it was certainly not so with these.

I have always strongly felt: "The most unmanly and despicable of males are those who abuse women physically or emotionally!"

After the doctor sewed up my head, put an antiseptic dressing on it; and wrapped Mary's swollen ankle they left saying, "I still think you had a fight."

Michael, who brought about the whole fiasco, slept through it all.

We often went for a Sunday drive, and when we were in an area where there were oil wells Michael was fascinated with them. When he saw one, he asked, "What's that?" We told him they were oil wells and were pumping oil. His fascination was with the rocking action of the walking beam that raised and lowered the pump cylinder.

Whenever he saw one working he would start chanting "El well pumpin doin doin!" "El well pumpin doin doin!" After a handful of repeats we would say, "Yes, Michael the oil well is pumping!" He would never let it go at that. He kept on chirping "El well pumpin doin doin".

We would say, "Yes, now don't say that anymore." We might as well have said it to the oil well.

Mary's dad, and people newly around Michael, often asked, "Did you have that kid vaccinated with a phonograph needle?"

In '43 Randy was born and Mary was soon busy with the raising of two kids who fought with each other much as had my brother and I.

She needed a break from the tedium so I took over in the evening so she could go to a bible study class of local women. With two small kids, one especially disruptive, we seldom went to church services.

After some searching, delayed by the wait for the kids to get big enough to stay with Mary's mother, we found that the pastor of the local Presbyterian Church shared our belief of Jesus as Savior, and as God with the Father and the Holy Spirit.

Pastor Bruce Kurrle led his congregation to that commitment.

In '51 Mary and I joined St. Johns Presbyterian Church on the out-skirts of Compton, where we met Virginia Fuller, and where she and Mary became "best friends". The three of us came to love the church and its people.

Mary felt I should spend some time with just the boys, and suggested that I could take them fishing. I went to the hardware store and bought fully equipped poles for the three of us and a jar of salmon eggs. The next morning I got them up at four and we took off for the Santa Ana River.

We got out of the car and started to walk to the river. A few steps into the treed area, I realized that we couldn't see well enough to not drop into a ravine. We went back to the car and sat there for about an hour and a half, before we groped our way through the underbrush to the river.

We caught no fish and the kids were tired and cranky. The fishing gear languished in the garage until we moved, when I gave it to the Salvation Army.

Michael found a turtle in the empty lot across the street, and made it his pet. He was lying on his back on the front lawn with his turtle on his chest.

The turtle thought the red meat looked like good eating. It snapped it's jaws on Michael's lower lip, and would have eventually gotten a good piece of meat; if our neighbor, Paul Mickel, hadn't used his pocket-knife to stab it in the throat.

Instead of being thankful, Michael was "mad" at Paul.

Virginia Fuller joined St. John's about the same time as Mary and I, and she and Mary, who were almost the same age, quickly became fast friends. They shared an interest in giving care to any in need, and kept in close touch for so long as they lived near each other.

We admired Virginia's caring and loving spirit, and had concern for her because her husband was an abusive and non-supportive; gun toting, heavy drinking, union business agent.

As we became more aware of those circumstances we tried to talk her into divorcing him, but Virginia resisted, "God doesn't approve of divorce."

But, when the abuse came to a point of violence, giving her much concern for Genna Sue's safety; she left with only personal belongings, including her daughter.

With the moral support of many of St. John's parishioners Virginia finally divorced her abusive and immoral gun-toting union business agent husband.

Even when John Fuller was sober, he hit her and held a gun to her head.

We felt that if she hadn't rid herself of him, she and her daughter might not have survived.

Now she at least didn't have to support his drinking habit. She had only to provide for her daughter and herself.

For many years Virginia had labored hard, at her profession of nursing; to provide everything her only child needed, and much that she didn't need but just wanted.

Genna Sue's was a pampered childhood. Virginia poured all her love into her only child.

Mary and I became acquainted with Genna Sue, when she and our son Randy dated.

Randy brought her to our Park Estates home one night, after taking her to see Hitchcock's "Psycho".

She was shivering so much that she needed to be quieted before taking her home to Virginia.

She sat on the family room sofa in front of the log fire with Mary's arm around her.

It took quite a while for the trembling to cease, then Randy took her home to Lynwood.

Virginia, Mary, and I were members of St. John's Cornerstone class, which was our sole social contact; but the two of them kept regularly in telephone touch and served together as deacons.

I served as a trustee and in '53 was ordained a Presbyterian elder.

One of my most cherished keepsakes is my leather bound Scofield Reference Bible.

It was presented to me at the annual banquet; and was inscribed inside the cover, "Carl Lodjic, President Cornerstone Class St. John's Presbyterian Church 1956."

Before joining St. John's I didn't really know what being a Christian meant, but I was now a full-fledged member of God's family.

My secular life was also changing; Pacific Iron's president, Howard Smits, moved me into an office job in the estimating department, but in a short time I asked to be returned to shop management because I preferred the "physically active".

However, Howard had hatched a plan for his future and for mine, so I was soon moved back into the office as Chief Estimator.

Next, I was moved into sales; which required being often away from home, since we had customers and jobs in progress in several states, and in Europe and the South Pacific.

I was logging more air travel miles than many airline pilots and was an honorary member of most VIP clubs, and became United Airlines first "Million Mile" member.

Morrison-Knudsen, one of the worlds largest construction firms, was a good customer of P.I., and their Los Angeles office was my territory.

Jim Wells was the manager of the L.A. office, and we became close friends. He was going to make a call on a job some distance away, and asked me to go with him in the company airplane; because P.I. might be interested in being the structural steel supplier.

The pilot had properly checked everything, and we took off from Mines Field. We had reached our cruising altitude when Jim heard a rattling sound, and realized that he had left his keys in the door of the plane. He didn't want to lose any time, so he suggested that I brace my feet against the opposite wall of the airplane and push hard enough for him to get his hand out to get the keys. I was able to exert enough pressure for him to retrieve them, but he broke the crystal on his watch.

When I related the incident to my friend and neighbor, who had the Cessna dealership at Long Beach, he convinced me that it was a stupid thing to do. "Jim might have been making a jump without parachute, and if the door had opened far enough for the wind to catch it, you would have made "the dive" together."

The next day I was booked on a United Airlines flight to New York, and was in the Los Angeles clubroom, waiting time for my flight departure.

I noticed, sitting across the room from me, Danny Kaye (Kubelski). I smiled and said "Hello". He glared at me with the look of: "Who do you think you are!"

At that point in life I was probably making many times as much as he, because "entertainers" were then paid what they are really worth; something less than janitors.

I was just trying to be polite; after all we're both Polacks, so I ignored the "snub".

Pacific Iron and Steel was a major contender for a contract to provide and erect one million square feet of warehouses for the armed forces in remote areas of the U.S. "protection zone".

Our sales manager had been in New York calling on the joint venture contractor and on the Corps of Engineers East Atlantic division. Each day he reported that he expected a contract the next day.

He had been living in the Sherry Netherlands hotel for six weeks and the hotel bill and other expenses mounted high.

Howard called me into his office and said, "You are now executive vice-president and as such you are to go to New York, fire our sales manager, and take over the effort to get that contract."

I didn't relish confrontation with the man who had been my immediate boss, but I did as I was told, and sent him back to Los Angeles where he cleaned out his desk and left the company.

Four days later, following around the clock conferencing with the Joint Venture manager and the Colonel who headed the East Atlantic Division of the Corps of Engineers, we were granted a contract.

I returned home bushed but triumphant.

The next morning, after having slept around the clock; I followed up a tip given to me by a friend in the Corps of Engineers, and called Strategic Air Command headquarters and asked for General Curtis LeMay. The operator said, "Who's calling?" I replied, in a somewhat sleepy voice, "Carl Lodjic".

His response of, "Yes, Colonel Lodjic, I'll patch you right through", was amusing but helpful!

Every subsequent time, I purposely slurred the "Carl Lodjic", and got the same response.

P.I. had re-designed, furnished, and erected the first B36 hangar at the SAC base near Albuquerque, New Mexico; and General LeMay wanted a duplicate in French Morrocco.

We fabricated and shipped it, and sent a superintendent and two foremen with it, who completed it within ninety days.

A few months later Howard called me into his office and said, "At our seminar, on the survey sheet, you indicated you would like to someday have your own steel fabricating company. I have other things in mind for myself so I want you to buy me out."

I then realized why Howard had been constantly promoting me; but I knew of no way that we could find the money to do so, because we had just moved into our new home in the Park Estates area of Long Beach.

Paying for the lot, architect fees, and construction; and furnishing of the three bedroom, three bath, house of brick and beveled plank redwood siding, with log burning fireplaces in both the living room and family room, took "every dime" we had. There was only enough left in our bank account to handle utility and food costs.

Money was so tight that Mary and I would go to the market together and, as she put item after item in the cart, I would mentally tally the total. With our limited budget I needed to be certain we were not overspending or overcharged.

As the checker entered digitally (with one finger) the amount for each item, I would tire of the slow process and say, "The total is $47.53." Mary would "shush" me, but I would repeat the total until the checker said, "$47.53 please".

With our financial resources so tight, I saw no way we could possibly buy out Howard; but he had it all pre-planned because of his strong desire for a large avocado acreage in Rancho Santa Fe, a short distance inland from San Diego. He let me use his P.I. stock certificate as loan collateral for the necessary $75,000 from the Bank of America.

A senior vice president of the main office branch in Los Angeles, who was a friend to both of us, handled the transaction.

In discussing the matter with Mary I could see she was extremely concerned about such a huge undertaking of debt but she said, "You've successfully handled the financial decisions so far, so I'll go along with whatever you decide."

I knew that if I defaulted we would be back to "square one", Howard would have the P.I. ownership back in his hands for whatever remained to be repaid on the loan, I would be his servant forever; and he would have his avocado ranch.

The few minor stockholders continued their ownership for a short time. With my fifty-one percent ownership I was able to have the company buy back the stock of any that left.

Although Mary and I were worried by the heavy debt we continued giving financial help to her folks and to mine.

The company prospered so well we were debt-free in two years time.

I took over the job of president and principal owner when I was thirty-seven, and at thirty-nine we placed the stock certificate in our safe deposit box.

We had been tithing for several years but now double-tithed.

Through David Packard introducing me to the Young President's Organization, I came to realize that I was the youngest president of a U.S. manufacturing corporation doing as large a dollar volume of business as was Pacific Iron and Steel Corporation of Los Angeles.

I joined YPO on Dave's suggestion and came to have such high regard for him that I hoped he would seek the office of President of our United States of America.

I felt that Dave, at that time a founding partner of Hewlett-Packard in the fledgling computer manufacturing industry, would be the best and most respected President in the history of our country.

Had we been able to continue a close relationship, I would have urged him to do so and would have spearheaded his candidacy; but we were both busy at our work places many miles apart.

Our Park Estates home had a six-foot tall grape stake fence around the back yard. A local dentist constructed a house with swimming pool on the lot behind our rear fence.

He soon put the house on the market and sold it to a handsome six-foot-four guy, named Roman Gabriel. Roman and his pretty blonde wife asked Michael if he would "pool sit" their two little boys.

Michael, who loved both swimming and football, was quick to oblige.

There was a giant of a man of color who visited the Gabriels quite often. "Rosie" (Roosevelt) Grier opened the holes for and protected

Roman when he quarterbacked for the Los Angeles Rams football team. "Rosie" went on to protect people in another way, when he became a Christian minister.

We often saw him entering Roman's house with a Bible under his arm.

Michael could have walked to California State-Long Beach, from our home in Park Estates; but instead commuted by VW bug. He graduated as a Physical Education major, but was not employable as a coach because he wasn't "degreed" in an academic subject that he could teach.

The college education we bought for him prepared him for nothing; but through my friendships he had several jobs with construction companies and with U.S. Steel and Kaiser Permanete Cement.

Randy entered Whittier College; Richard Nixon's alma mater in Whittier, California; where Nixon lived and where he was a partner in the law firm of Newley, Knoop & Nixon.

Randy stayed on campus where he had a roommate named Richard who lived with his folks about a block from us in Park Estates. Richard was studying to enter the medical profession.

Mary and I took the two of them to lunch at Coco's restaurant, and Richard was telling us how he was going to have a difficult time repaying his folks for the cost of his education.

Randy related privately how insurmountable a load this was on Richard.

During the drive home Mary and I discussed the matter.

The next day I called my vice-president friend at Bank of America and told him of our desire to present five-thousand-dollars to Richard anonymously.

He had the paperwork prepared, and met with me at the California Club, where I took him to lunch and signed the necessary papers.

Included was a letter to Richard stating that the donor was giving the money for him to use to retire his educational debt.

About a week later I saw Richard driving down our street in a new BMW.

This was the first of several times that I was a patsy, but I'd rather err in that direction than to ignore someone in need.

Being not Pharisees, we didn't tell Randy about the gift to Richard, lest he feel responsible.

After graduating from Whittier College, Randy entered San Anselmo Theological Seminary in San Anselmo, California. He was to become a Presbyterian minister.

I wanted him to study theology at Princeton but Mary wanted him close to home and Randy quickly bought that idea.

While he was in school at San Anselmo he married Phylis Jean in our St. John's Presbyterian Church in Compton, where Michael had previously married Linda. Virginia Fuller was hostess at both receptions. As Mary's closest friend and her fellow deacon we were pleased that she took part in the wedding of each of our kids.

In our desire to restrict the "too-rapidly growing" population of "Baby Boomers", and thereby reduce human misery and crime, we urged our sons to follow my example with vasectomies.

Both had the operation after producing two children. Randy later had a reversal when he re-married, following a failed first marriage, which produced one child to replace his new wife.

We survived, our kids survived, our grand kids survived; and we did our part to save the world while much of the rest of it "marched madly on" cranking out kids.

Unfortunately governments use our tax money to foster a wanton attitude by giving tax incentives to those who continue to crank them out like peanuts.

It would cost the taxpayers far less, and our world would more likely survive until the last days, if they instead, provided vasectomies free to any married couple who had already produced two offspring and could not afford the operation.

With the collapse of morality, overpopulation continued exceptionally rapid growth; bringing about an alarming increase in crime!

Much of that rapid increase came from the new habit of living together without marriage.

This new way of life started in '57 with the "Baby Boomers", and became more prevalent as the years went by.

In '57, P.I. had a workforce of fifteen hundred, and was breaking volume and performance records.

I was now forty, and had been working for a living twenty-eight years.

The minimum wage when I started to work was twenty-five cents an hour. On this my fortieth birthday, little more than a quarter century later, the minimum wage was increased to one dollar per hour for all but farm workers; an increase of four-hundred percent!

"Work less and get paid more"; was the "baby boomer" philosophy that brought on the "work habit" of less exertion, and the "eat habit" of more stuffing.

1957 and '58 were new depression years for the construction industry; so the independent steel fabricating companies faced extremely tough competition from mill-owned fabricators, making it difficult to survive.

Bethlehem Steel Company, United States Steel Company and Kaiser Steel Company all had their own fabricating shops, giving them the advantage of the assured profit from the sale of the mill product. Also the "mill-owned" fabricators had the additional advantage of paying sales tax on their cost of raw materials for the mill product; while the independents had to pay on the fabricated selling price.

Our government, instead of protecting the little guys, favored the big.

When the mark-up of profit was reduced to almost nothing to win contracts, independents such as P.I., had to be super-efficient to overcome the mill fabricator advantages.

To have the low bid we couldn't add more than three percent for contingencies and profit. One slip and we would be in the red!

No entity can survive without profit, so we had to use our ingenuity.

In an attempt to overcome the "mill fabricator" competition's unfair advantage, I met the top brass of Union Pacific Railway in a special dining room atop the Hotel Utah in Salt Lake City. When the waiter took our lunch orders he also took "mixer" orders from my new Mormon friends. They had each brought along a paper sack that they put under the table containing their own private stock.

In spite of my aversion to booze, I purchased from them a large industrial acreage in Ogden, Utah and installed a fabricating plant there to give P.I. the freight cost advantage called, "fabrication in transit".

It did the trick for us in the tight times but profits were still so small that any slight inefficiency would spell loss.

Innovative fixtures and automated operations gave us the needed efficiency, but with demand so low many independents still wouldn't survive. I wanted to make certain we were not one of them!

I went on the lookout for a proprietary metal product that, with our expertise and equipment, we could efficiently handle. We had been manufacturers of large hangar doors for aircraft garaging, so were capable of design and manufacture of motorized steel items. Perhaps we could find other items along that line.

United Airlines was one of our best customers for these huge doors, so I was in the office of Seely Hall, senior vice president, to negotiate another contract for hangars and hangar doors.

I had with me Carvel Moore, our industrial designer and illustrator. Carvel had become friends with Seely through his previous employment with Douglas Aircraft Company.

Seely's phone rang and he excused himself to take the call. His natural way of talking was with the use of four letter words interspersed with a few others. The cussing grew more and more frequent and heated. When he finished I said, "What was that all about?"

He related that they had signed a contract with Lockheed Air Services to design and to produce a device that would board passengers direct from the second level of the terminal through a tunnel to the aircraft passenger door. The present conversation was to the effect that the contract, which called for $50,000.00 for engineering and $50,000.00 for each unit installed on the terminal building, was being amended by Lockheed to $100,000.00 for engineering and $100,000.00 for each unit.

It was a joint contract with United and American. Each had budgeted for 90 gates. The outlay of each was to be $50,000.00 plus ninety times $50,000.00 for the installed units; a total of $4,550,000.00.

Seely had a call from the same party about two weeks prior saying the price was adjusted to $75,000.00 for engineering plus $75,000.00 for each unit; a total of $6,825,000.00, a 50% increase.

Now he was being told, "The price is $100,000.00 for engineering and $100,000.00 for each unit." The increase was 100%!

How could anyone expect a favorable response when they even lacked the inventiveness to avoid using the round figure increment of $25,000.00?

That's more insulting than the all too common use of something on sale at $199,999.99.

In the construction business, increases of more than 5% were unheard of; and always had to be substantiated in detail, and initiated by a change in customer requirements.

I told Seely, "They need to be forced to put down the blunt pencil. You need to find a competitor to Lockheed." He agreed and asked, "Do you have anyone in mind?"

I said, "I might", and asked, "Do you have definitive drawings of what L.A.S. has in mind?" "No but we have a plywood mock-up over at O'Hare. I'll get a driver for you, if you're really interested."

The driver took us to O'Hare, which at that time wasn't Chicago's commercial field. We looked with wonderment at the four pieces of plywood nailed together and attached to an opening in what represented a wall; and were dumbfounded at how little Lockheed had done for their $50,000 engineering charge.

We went back to Seely's office where I assured him we could produce a better answer at a lesser price, and asked, "Can you assure me that you can cancel with Lockheed and award Pacific Iron the contract if our proposal serves your need at a lesser price?"

He called the company lawyer and gave us the assurance, but told us they were making the final decision in just two weeks, and must have a formal proposal with concept drawings, by that time.

This seemed to be the answer to my quest.

In '57 the flight time from Chicago Midway to Los Angeles International was eight hours. While I described how the thing would work and how it might look, Carvel drew out the "Jetway", as our copyrighted name would be. When we landed at LAX, he had a free hand presentation drawing that was as good or better than most drafting tool pictures. From that drawing we could estimate costs and time schedule, and Carvel could make the presentation drawings.

Carvel and I burned the midnight oil for the next ten days; and gave Seely a firm proposal of $57,000.00 per unit, plus freight cost, at all stations within the contiguous United States. We guaranteed that the mating to the aircraft passenger door would service all present commercial aircraft, and that the Jetway would automatically align with the aircraft floor as the aircraft rose or descended from the unloading or loading of passengers.

Contract terms provided for an automatic increase tied to the Consumers Price Index of "cost of living", when and if it rose more than three percent.

Since we were making no charge for engineering and development, the contract was to have a clause guaranteeing that all such equipment, if it served the physical needs, would be purchased exclusively from Pacific Iron & Steel Corporation of L.A., for so long as P.I. was willing and could produce.

Since we later sold to all airlines, we had to remove that language from our standard contract.

It was time for me to follow the example of my favorite Old Testament character, Joshua!

In Joshua 6:20 he created havoc for the enemy, and fought and won the battle of Jericho against overwhelming odds.

I became Jetway Joshua, against overwhelming odds, as I fought the battle for Jetway against the corporate giants: Lockheed, Stanray, and Eero Sarinnen (Architect for Dulles International Airport); and became its creator!

I was blest to have in my "army"; Robert Lichti, a brilliant young structural engineer who designed it with the help of his friend Morley English, professor of structural engineering at UCLA, where they had access to a computer.

I was also blest to have Robert Campbell who managed the Ogden facility that was originally our secondary steel fabricating plant, which we converted into the Jetway plant.

The first twelve were installed at Idylwild in New York for United Airlines.

The "fabrication in transit" freight rate saved a lot of money, because Jetways have since been installed at every major airport for every major airline throughout the world.

My little creation was but as a drop in His oceans when I contemplate all God created in just six days; and each day the result was immediately viewable!

As Jetway Joshua, I gave it all I had; but it took six months to view the first result.

My Score two ended at 1:06+am on May 9, 1957.

Score 3

(1:07am May 9, 1957 thru 1:06+am May 9, 1977)

Taxing years.

Dwight David Eisenhower was re-elected President of these United States by a landslide. With such acceptance he put the brakes on the inflation that is so ruinous to retired people who are on fixed income. Increased wages and increased prices take a huge bite of the savings that were put aside to cover "retirement years".

I was concerned, not only for my folks and Mary's folks; but for all retired persons; because costs are often double or triple those of their earnings years; and additionally require greater spending for medical needs. Their only help would have to come through income tax relief.

Replacing the Income Tax with a National Sales Tax would bring equity to all. The more you spend the more you pay.

What could possibly be simpler and fairer?

Yet, fair or not, politicians resist because much of their financial backing comes from the rich, who are the big spenders and the big contributors at campaign time.

It was hoped that Ike's clout could swing it, and perhaps our representatives could be persuaded to vote other than their pocketbook; but it didn't happen.

In my fortieth year on this planet, John Glenn set a new intercontinental speed record, flying from my hometown of Long Beach, California to Mom's hometown of Brooklyn, New York; in three hours and twenty-three minutes! Celebration of that was followed by a mammoth fireworks display with the first underground atomic explosion, in the desert near Boulder City, Nevada.

These events were overshadowed by the devastating racial violence in Little Rock, Arkansas.

President Eisenhower ordered 1000 paratroopers to enforce the desegregation of Central High School.

The hardly noticed other bad news was that the average wages for factory workers was now $2.08 per hour, $83.20 per week; an all time high, bringing even more inflation!

Labor union pressure was too much for Congress.

The Los Angeles Illustrated Daily News reported the good news that there was a definite link of lung cancer to smoking. Now the problem was in getting people to accept the finding and to give up the habit that made them stink and brought them a horrible lingering death.

I tried several times to quit by cutting down each day from the number smoked the day before, but always fell back to my pack a day habit. But, with this news and the news of damage to the innocently exposed, I decided to quit for my family's sake. The effort strained my will power mightily but I finally made the grade, and never regressed as I was strengthened in my resolve by the painful lingering death of friends and acquaintances who kept on smoking.

Being completely engrossed in the development and marketing of Jetways helped me kick the habit, so I tell others who are straining, "If you really want to quit, keep super busy and get over-involved in good deeds!"

Jetway development benefited me, both physically and financially; and continues to benefit all persons who travel by air. But none appreciate them as much as those in wheelchairs, and especially those who had in past years boarded or deplaned using a moveable stairs; often walking across the apron through blizzards or dust storms!

With Jetway contracts from United Airlines and American, and contracts pending from Continental, TWA, Delta, Pan-Am, Braniff, and Western; Pacific Iron and Steel Corp. of L.A. got the attention of corporate giants who visualized the big profit figures and wanted to enlarge and diversify.

A commercial broker from Chicago called for an appointment to discuss the purchase of Pacific Iron. He represented Standard Railway Equipment Manufacturing Company of Chicago and asked, "Would Pacific Iron be for sale if the price was right?"

Stanray, as they would soon be called on the New York Stock Exchange, was a large company that manufactured railway equipment and in a diversification program had recently acquired the Arkansas Traveler Boat manufacturing company of Little Rock, Arkansas.

With the efforts of a $1,000,000.00 per year Research and Development department they had expected to get contracts from the airlines for their "people loaders".

Our Research and Development budget was non-existent, but we were imaginative and inventive!

Tom Patterson, United Airlines president contracted with the best for his company, contrary to popular belief that executives will deal unfairly to benefit personal friends, such as were the presidents of Stanray and of United Airlines.

Since his business and golfing relationship didn't pay off; Stanray's president, Art Williams, decided that the best way to get in the "people loader" business was to acquire the winner, so he sent a Chicago broker to ask about the availability of Pacific Iron and Steel Corporation of L. A.

I told the broker I would check with the other stockholders, and would meet with him at the California Club at nine o'clock the next morning.

My joy was in creating something beneficial to mankind, not in being a billionaire, so I told him we were agreed that if the price and terms were right we would sell. He contacted Art Williams, who gave him an offer price. After a few telephone conversations, the price was raised to an acceptable figure and the sale was consummated. Jetway Joshua again felt the exhilaration of winning the battle.

Mary and I double-tithed our portion of the sale proceeds to St. John's Church for a new sanctuary, offices, and classroom building, so I gained the job of Building Committee Chairman, and was again a multi-job entrepreneur. We hired a Long Beach architect with whom I worked on the plans, and hired a contractor who built a 750-seat sanctuary with offices and classrooms. The pastor loved it and said the acoustics were so good you could hear a pin drop.

We were amused by a crusty and retired old real estate agent, who grudgingly gave a minimal contribution; but cried tears of joy the Sunday morning that we first met in the new sanctuary, and loudly proclaimed, "My church"!

My everyday job didn't change because the terms of sale required me to remain as president of Pacific Iron and to become a member of the Stanray Board of Directors. In 1960 I began monthly trips to Chicago for Friday management meetings and Monday Board of Directors meetings. When added to all of the other business travel, this was an unwelcome chore that I nonetheless dutifully carried out.

Sunday mornings in Chicago found me in worship service at First Presbyterian Church on Michigan Avenue, where the ushers wore tuxedos, and where I quickly found that I could not just walk down the aisle and sit where I wanted. It was an exclusive clique.

Some of my travel was on chartered small aircraft because it was the best means for me to visit jobs in progress. Whenever it worked into the flight plan I visited the Ogden plant which was under the capable leadership of my friend Bob Campbell; a registered Civil Engineer, and ex-Navy officer.

On one such sortie I had with me my government contracts administrator, retired Brigadier General Charles H. (Chick) McNutt, and my field superintendent Frank Lipis.

I had previously chartered planes with a friend and neighbor who had a fleet of twin engine Cessnas and of Bell Helicopters at the nearby Long Beach airport.

Those flights had been perfect and without incident, even when we encountered bad weather; but this time I let my Assistant Pastor, Ted Nissen, talk me into trying his friend who was a commercial airline pilot and owned a Piper Apache.

We flew from Mines Field Los Angeles to Montgomery Field San Diego where we were erecting the structural steel for a high rise building.

The next leg took us over the Las Vegas "strip" as we traveled to Provo, Utah, where we were installing an industrial building.

When we were directly over the "strip" both engines cut out. Our pilot began feverishly checking and flipping buttons and handles.

Looking down between his seat and mine I noticed we had taken off on the auxiliary tank. I switched it over to the main tank and the engines responded immediately.

"Lone Eagle" looked utterly confused, so I told him what had happened. He was embarrassed and thanked me as we proceeded uneventfully to Provo; although we had lost the functioning of all instruments.

We visited our Provo crew that was erecting the structure of a new manufacturing plant. Progress was on schedule, so we were there only a few hours.

Our next leg was a short one from Provo to Ogden where we visited the Jetway plant. Bob Campbell and his staff and crew were efficiently busy.

We lunched with Bob and his plant superintendent, Walter Burns; then Bob drove us back to the airport for our flight to The Dalles, Oregon where we were erecting the buildings for the Harvey Aluminum Company aluminum production mill.

Shortly after leaving Ogden the weather got extremely rough. We bounced around like a cork on a windswept sea. Although we had no instruments to aid us, the visibility was good enough for us to make it safely to The Dalles airport.

I had negotiated the contract with the Harvey family to design furnish fabricate and erect all of the structural steel for their new mill. Our guaranteed maximum was $2,000,000.00, with their actual cost based on 5 % profit added to our out of pocket cost. After the contract was formalized I learned that our guaranteed maximum was considerably below American Bridge's quotation, so Harvey knew they had a good deal!

If, upon completion, the cost (including the 5% profit) was less than the guaranteed maximum, P.I. would return half of the excess to Harvey.

As part of the "wrap-up package" to be presented to Mr. Leo Harvey, I had arranged with a friend, who had a Publicity, Advertising, and Public Relations firm in Los Angeles to meet us at the job and take job photos from the air.

Earl Witscher didn't show up until the next day and I was somewhat irritated. I berated him for his tardiness.

He said, "Boss, I did the best I could, with this weather I couldn't find a pilot willing to fly me here from Portland in an open-sided plane from which I could take the aerials. I finally got this one drunk enough to do it but I had to spend several hours in a bar with him before he would agree. He gave me the flight of my life. We flew under every bridge over the Columbia River between Portland and here. Now, what else do you want me to photograph?"

I apologized and the next day Earl flew back to Portland with his aerial cameras and his "new found" pilot friend.

We received signed acceptance by Harvey's job manager and I presented Leo Harvey, for his half of the savings, a $250,000.00 check. He smiled and graciously accepted. But, a few seconds later he was loudly berating me for making $250,000.00 more than I had expected; but his ire was short lived and we continued to be friends.

The next day we prepared to leave The Dalles.

Our pilot was ready to take us to Sacramento, California where we were erecting a huge sugar beet storage building we had designed and fabricated for a sugar co-op at nearby Woodland.

Lone Eagle cleared with the control tower for safe skies in a south-westerly route over Mt. Hood, which we would need to avoid, because her height was more than our Piper Apache ceiling.

We would also need continuing good visibility as we were still without instruments.

About fifteen minutes out of The Dalles the weather got so rough that the plane was being violently "wracked about" with cracks and groans that indicated excessive stressing. Visibility was absolute zero.

This was no fun for us, and our pilot of eleven years commercial experience, passed out!

None of us had flight instruction so we just held the wheel steady while my companions in the back seat slapped and shook him and began to administer oxygen to arouse him. He came to just as we looked down through a clearing in the clouds and saw The Dalles airport, that we had left a very long fifteen to twenty minutes before.

Without calling the tower, that had sent us out in that stuff, he nosed down and abruptly landed us back at The Dalles.

We would not take off again until conditions bettered so I got a room for Lone Eagle, one for Chick and Frank, and one for me, at the local motel. We bedded down for the night somewhat exhausted.

At six the next morning I knocked on our pilots door. He sleepily answered and said he would be ready in a few minutes.

Having second thoughts, I had other plans. I said, "Get your sleep and go back whenever you want, we're driving to Portland and going back commercial. Send me your bill."

That was the last and only time I used my assistant pastor's friend, so we survived; doubtless aided by the Lord through Mary's prayers, which she later told me were going heavenward at the very time we were in the most difficult of circumstances.

I was forty-three when Art Williams, Chairman of the Board of what was now called Stanray, and I went to England, France, Italy, Germany, Holland, and Switzerland to enter into contracts with representatives to market and install Jetways in Europe.

After thorough background checks we contracted with one based in England for sales there; and with one in Switzerland for European continent sales and installations.

The London representative picked us up at Heathrow airport in his Rolls Royce. He took us sightseeing and then to his exclusive men's Pub for libation and food, where I was introduced to "white bait"; deep-fried whole minnows!

We formalized our agreement with him and he took us back to our hotel. When he transported us to the airport the next morning for our flight to Paris, he said, "I'll wire you my flight number and estimated time of arrival for my Jetway plant tour, and would be most pleased if you can take the time to show me Disneyland."

The other chosen representative was a "race car" driver and member of a royal family. His wife was heiress to the Nestle Chocolate fortune. He picked us up in his sports car at Paris and drove us through the Chateau country where we visited the "cathedrals of fame"; and then took us to Munich where Art and I each bought a new Mercedes to be delivered to our closest U.S. seaport.

After we made our car purchases he drove us to a castle overlooking Lake Geneva in Switzerland; where he and his wife lived. It was beautiful, rivaling the architecture of the cathedrals, but uninviting and cold. We spent the night there and formalized our agreement.

He drove us to the airport in Bern from where we flew Swissair back to New York. Art stayed in the company apartment in downtown Manhattan. I flew home to Los Angeles.

A few weeks later I picked up our London representative at LAX and hosted him to a day at Disneyland, before indoctrinating him in the details of Jetways. He was formally attired so I wore a dark business suit and tie to make him comfortable. It must have been quite a sight as two business-suited men, one with an eight inch twirled mustache, rode together on Disneyland's Matterhorn.

A new Board of Directors member named Hal Kibbey, brother of an actor named Guy, came on board at Stanray soon after my return from Europe. I was introduced to him in The University Club where I usually stayed in Chicago. Hal had been president of a small steel fabricating firm in Pocatello, Idaho. He was a tall distinguished man of erect stature who soon convinced Art that this rather plain appearing guy should be replaced by his golfing and drinking buddy who was a salesman for Kaiser Steel Company's fabricating division.

I didn't fit their mold. I was neither drinker nor golfer.

I was relieved of my job; and relieved to leave that high rolling bunch.

My friend Bob Campbell, who had known Kibbey as our competitor in the steel fabricating business, quit as soon as I was fired. Stanray had to quickly find a new Jetway manager!

I had purchased controlling interest in a small firm that designed, manufactured and sold automatic adjuster for air-braked vehicles such as heavy trucks and buses.

Heavy rigs wore the brake lining so quickly that the driver was required to make frequent stops to crawl under the equipment for manual adjustments. For this purpose there are truck-stop areas along major highways, especially in long downgrade areas, where there are also runaway emergency ramps.

After redesigning the devices and building the volume to be an attractive acquisition to a major company in the heavy vehicle-braking industry, I sold my little Autoset Company to a national firm called Gustin-Bacon. I had the joy of again creating something beneficial to mankind and made a small profit and again retired.

I had an office in Torrance, California owned by a partner in property development. Charlie Cake purchased property and developed it for sale or rental.

Bob MacDonald, my legal advisor and Executive Vice-president at Pacific Iron, Phil Lotz of Joslyn Manufacturing Company, Chicago, and I, formed a partnership with Charlie.

We purchased the property for, and built ninety-six two story triplex units to sell to people wanting a home and income.

Also we purchased a section of land across from the Torrance City Hall where we built and managed an office complex. The three of us provided the money and Charlie did the developing and managing.

One morning Charlie's secretary buzzed me and said, "There's a man named Hal Kibbey on the line." I had her put it through to my extension.

Hal had dethroned Art Williams as Chairman of the Board of Directors of Stanray. He was quite a toppler!

He began the conversation with an apology for having made the mistake of replacing me with his friend from Kaiser Steel. Lou had no management ability.

Then he asked if I would consider making a survey of the Pacific Iron and Steel fabricating operation, and advise him as to what action he should take to stop the losses. He said, "We've had a loss of over a million dollars each of the four years you've been gone."

After a lengthy conversation I agreed to drive up to Pacific Iron the next day if he would prepare the way by calling ahead and making arrangements to assure cooperation of the Chief Accountant, and of the Superintendent. He agreed.

After two days of talking to my old employees and of observing the shop operations I called Hal. I said, "You can expect at least a million cash from liquidation; and this is the only way to go since Lou has given the store away to the union with top-heavy wage rates and loss of efficiency control".

Many businesses have gone on the auction block, with the loss of many jobs, because of union intrusion into "management".

I called Hal and told him, "The property could be sold to a group who had federal funds to aid "Black American" business. Auctioneer Milt Wershow would sell the buildings and equipment at auction, and the field operation and its equipment, because of its record of profitability, could be sold separately.

Hal agreed to the plan and offered me a fee to manage it for him. I went to work the next morning. Hal had fired his old friend and I took back my old job of president.

Then began the task of completing the contracts that were on the books.

Keeping the work force energized, intact, and efficient; for seven months was difficult. Fortunately most of my old and loyal employees were still there and liked having me back.

We were fabricating the major columns for the twin tower Word Trade Center in New York. These were the mammoth supports that saved the Center and it's occupants when it was later sabotaged with explosives!

I worked myself out of a job on May 9, 1968 when I closed the door to my empty office.

I had been in the steel fabricating business exactly 32 years.

But this time I couldn't retire because I had a new job. I sold the erection business and it's equipment to an old friend and onetime toughest competitor, Austin Paddock, contingent upon my being president of the enterprise.

Paddy knew me as an opponent when he was president of American Bridge Company, the fabricating and erection arm of United States Steel Corporation, but he was now Chairman of the Board of Blount Brothers Construction of Montgomery, Alabama. Blount Brothers was a large General Contracting firm and Winton "Red" Blount had been Chairman of the Board.

In order to avoid conflict of interest speculation, "Red" resigned and appointed Paddy in his stead; when President Nixon appointed "Red" to the position of Postmaster General.

Such thinking was consistent with the cautious actions of the Richard Nixon that I came to know when he was a partner in the Whittier, California law firm of Newley, Knoop, and Nixon.

Mr. Nixon had been instrumental in bringing a Mr. Malaxa and his male secretary, Fred, out of Romania at the time of the Communist takeover. Mr. Malaxa was able to bring his considerable fortune with him to the United States and wanted to build a seamless steel tubing manufacturing plant in Southern California. Pacific Iron was interested in designing and constructing the plant so we met together in Nixon's office.

For reasons unknown to me, the project was abandoned following several meetings, and I never again met personally with Richard Milhous Nixon, but now I was working for his Postmaster General.

My new company was called Global Erectors, with headquarters in a rented facility on Signal Hill in Long Beach, California. Blount Brothers, in this diversification acquisition, paid Stanray $250,000 for the equipment and expertise and for the contracts that were left over at Pacific Iron and Steel.

Within two months, the purchase price was returned to Blount through the payments from those contracts.

Global's first new contract was to furnish and erect all of the structural steel for the new Cedars Sinai Hospital in Beverly Hills, California. We were well along with the erection of the structure when the President of Blount Brothers Construction prevailed upon Paddy to replace this California Yankee with a young southerner from his office.

By mutual agreement, I was relieved of my seven-year contract to run Global.

I was delighted to no more have to fly back and forth between Seattle, Washington (to visit my wife Mary for long weekends at our home in Gig Harbor) and Long Beach, California to tend the running of Global.

When I retired from the "automatic brake adjuster" business, Mary and I purchased a home on a small acreage in Gig Harbor. The move was at the insistence of our son Michael who was living there with his wife and children in a rented house at the end of the bay. Michael had been looking for a place to buy and had looked at this place but felt the house was too small for the four of them, but that it would be just right for our retirement home. He helped Mary move in while I was at work in my office on Signal Hill.

In 1972 the Dow Jones average closed above 1000 for the first time in history, and twenty-five years later it would close at 11,000. That's real "run away inflation"!

Although I had never taken an interest in that form of gambling, my friend Bob MacDonald suggested I buy some Montgomery-Ward stock, because they had just installed a new more progressive president.

It began a long gradual decline until, after holding it 4 years, I sold my $10,000 investment for $1,000 and never gambled again!

On my birthday in 1973 I retired for the fourth time to become a full time farmer of our little acreage in Gig Harbor, but Michael was again without a job and had no prospects so I went back in business.

Michael's major business experience was in employment services, so I purchased a franchise from Acme Personnel and established an office in Port Orchard, Washington; just across the bay from Bremerton where the Puget Sound Navy Shipyard is located.

It was only a few miles up the peninsula from Gig Harbor but because of the shortage of gasoline, due to the oil producing Arab's greed and their desire to punish what they called "the evil empire", I traded Mary's '67

Toronado for 2 Honda Civics. I received $175.00 as trade-in value on the purchase of the 2 Civics. It had cost me $7,000.00 and was in showroom condition with less than 20,000 miles on the odometer.

Michael and I tried to make a go of the Acme office but the employment market was so flat I closed it after one year of trying. One good thing came from it however: Michael got a job with General Electric Company's Credit office in the Southcenter area of Seattle.

With the new Civic that I had given him he had an economical car to drive and a not too distant commute.

The Acme venture cost me $20,000 but thankfully provided another job for Michael.

Since they lived nearby, Mary and I spent much of our free time with Michael and Linda and their children Rahna and Ric. We took them on vacations to such places as the Hallmark Inn at Cannon Beach, Oregon and the Awahnee Hotel in Yosemite, and regularly to some of our areas best restaurants.

Occasionally we took them to a movie, although neither Mary nor I had respect for overpaid entertainment personalities, so avoided them as much as possible.

Some "pro" athletes became entertainment personalities and got outrageous with long hair and ponytails or with weird hair coloring. Some also began getting salaries that should've been reserved for deserving people who made a contribution to the benefit of mankind.

So I also avoided patronizing pro football, basketball and baseball; and to help lower the Nielsen rating of Pro sports, quit watching them on TV.

Copying those "entertainment" personalities, some "males" began wearing the hairstyles and jewelry of women; and some women began wearing tattoos, emulating some of the female "outre" entertainers.

The Baby Boomers and their off spring brought about "she males" and other very undesirable changes. Distinguishing from the rear, which are female and which "she-male" is difficult. Hopefully the cycle will turn to bring back the days of "men are men and women are women".

Whatever happened to the desire to appear attractive, neat, and clean?

Maybe these outlandish persons will even give up the silly habit of wearing beaked sport caps and putting them on backwards.

To avoid such "people" we stopped patronizing any establishment where such creatures were employed; and sought out places where they were not.

We thoroughly enjoy our grand-kids and fortunately they enjoy us. They have often stated that their fondest memories are of when we took them out to eat or on vacation.

A few of my fondest memories are: When Rahna was with us she came running into the house all excited and said, "Poppa, airplanes scratching our sky!" Contrails were a new discovery for her.

And, when Michael and Linda were living in Kansas City where he was working for Western Girl, Mary and I flew back to see them and rented a car at the airport; as we pulled in their driveway, Ric stepped out on the porch with "Poppa, don't bang the buik!"

The "buik" was the new Skylark that we had bought them when they left California for Kansas. Perhaps his dad had gotten on him for banging into the car with his bicycle.

The first of the several times that we took them to the Hallmark Resort in Cannon Beach, Oregon; I was lying on the floor on my back and Rahna was sitting on my chest.

I feigned being dead and Rahna pushed my eyelids open with, "Poppa, are you in there?" She wouldn't give it up until I picked her up and hugged her to me.

Now we were living a few miles apart and would see them more often.

In my new job as small farm operator I was sentenced to a yearly six months of good "body building" labor. I rotor-tilled our half-acre garden area and spread composted chicken manure on it every Lincoln's birthday. We raised vegetables of all kinds, berries of several kinds, and a great deal of rhubarb. We also had an orchard of five varieties of apples and two of cherries, and nine blueberry bushes that produced berries the size of "jaw-breakers".

All had to be pruned, sprayed and fertilized several times a year.

We planted, nurtured and harvested all of our produce and distributed much of it to friends and a large amount to Peninsula Fish for needy families.

The community help organization was appropriately named "Peninsula Fish", from the biblical account of the dividing of two fish into enough to feed the multitude.

The lawn in front of the house was almost a half-acre in size and for several years I mowed it with a push mower. There was a pond between the front of the lawn and the orchard, that had running water which I piped down from springs in the forested area at the top rear of the acreage. I piped the overflow from the pond to the drainage ditch, alongside the road in front of the orchard, where we had a great crop of watercress. The pond and ditch required periodic attention to remove the moss.

With all this to attend to, it was retirement of a different sort but good for my body.

Mary and I wanted to help others by being problem solvers so we took a "Master Gardeners" course at the Washington State University experimentation campus in Puyallup, Washington.

We became certified master gardeners and represented the Pierce County Extension Service at booths in local garden shops where we helped people with their lawn and garden problems.

We also studied to be, and became, Laubach teachers of people who had English language problems. We spent two nights a week teaching

English to a Korean couple, but they were so interested in maintaining the Korean identity in their two children that the progress was negligible. After three years with them we gave it up at the suggestion of our supervisor. They wanted the benefits of citizenship, but wouldn't work at learning the language to get it.

Through the next four years, during the six months when there was no garden activity, I designed and single-handedly built a diesel-powered 24' boat. It had a stand-up shower, and a lavatory and head with an on-board waste processor. It slept six full size persons and had a galley with pantry, sink, and propane range and refrigerator.

I constructed it in the new garage I had a local contractor build for us, and hoisted the completed hull onto a new boat trailer and pulled it out of the garage.

The garage door opening wouldn't accommodate the full height of the boat so I built the cabin sole separately, hoisted it onto my pickup truck and moved it out of the garage and onto the hull section. Then, on the new boat trailer, I completed the fiberglass joining of the two sections.

I stood back and admired my "single handed" creation of four years duration and was anxiously looking forward to launching her and trying out the unique hull design, the new Isuzu diesel marine engine, and the jet drive auxiliary gasoline outboard.

When I checked out the procedure for first launch I found the red tape with the U.S. Coast Guard, Washington State Police, and Gig Harbor police, to be overwhelming!

I called the Tacoma Sea Scouts, and offered them a new diesel powered 24' cruiser on a new boat trailer. They arrived in about 45 minutes with a properly equipped pickup truck.

I didn't need the tax deduction, so my satisfaction came from the delight of the Sea scouts.

This was my third creation, and closed another life chapter that began when I bought my first of three new boats in '73.

I was now sixty years young and no longer interested in boats or in any other "adult toys".

The day the boat was towed away I decided to trim off the tent caterpillar infestation from three white birches in our front yard. I used a 12-foot-tall, three-legged orchard ladder from which I could reach the infested parts if I stood on the top with my pruning pole. I had trimmed off a few places when the ladder began to topple. It was leaning toward dropping me on top of a ten foot diameter, hundred-year-old fir that had been trimmed into a ball shape, and had many spiky branches ready to impale me.

I tossed the pruning pole as far as I could and jumped.

In jumping from that height I twisted my back and ankle.

I crawled across the huge lawn and to the front door and banged against it. Mary heard the noise and came to investigate. She dragged me inside and called 911. The paramedics of our Fire Department soon arrived and made a hasty examination on our living room floor. The fire captain who was a friend of ours wanted to take me to emergency at a hospital in Tacoma. I persisted in non-cooperation and was allowed to recuperate at home.

At 60, I needed to be a bit more cautious and especially to ascertain that none of a ladder's legs is atop a mole tunnel.

Perhaps the injury brought on the shingles that I broke out with the next day.

Live and learn. With the Lord's help I did both.

My score three ended at 1:06+am May 9, 1977 when I passed through the "taxing years".

Score 4

1:07am May 9, 1977 thru 1:07+am May 9, 1997

Saddening years.

Michael's wife, Linda, had been experiencing persistent discomfort to the extent that she finally went to our family doctor for a check-up.

Doctor Quiring sent her to an Oncologist who confirmed she had Leukemia.

It quickly took its toll and she began Chemotherapy treatments. Her once trim body soon became "puffy", and she lost all her hair. Her only hope was for a bone marrow transplant.

The only likely donor was her brother, a high school teacher in Long Beach, but Linda vetoed having the transplant.

We took care of all Linda's medical and burial expenses to alleviate Michael's trials.

During the time Linda was undergoing therapy we paid Michael's tuition and expenses to return to college at the University of Puget Sound to get a degree in something that might establish a career.

He had never been fired but went through thirteen jobs in nine years, mostly arranged for by me.

Mercifully our Linda lasted only a short time. It was a difficult time for Michael, Rahna, and Ric; and for Mary and I, who thought of her and loved her as the daughter we never had.

Since Michael and Linda had stopped going to any church, we arranged for a simple memorial service at our Presbyterian Church in Gig Harbor.

Linda was cremated and buried at a cemetery in Gig Harbor in a plot that Mary and I had purchased for future needs.

At the University of Puget Sound Michael met a young lady who was a professor's assistant in one of his classes. She was the same age as his daughter but they hit it off and soon asked us to arrange for them to be married in our Chapel Hill church. Neither Michael nor bride Elizabeth was a member, but Mary and I had been for years.

At this marriage, for the first time in the lives of our kids, Virginia didn't act as hostess. She had re-married and was living in Phelan, California; but Mary kept her advised, sharing with her all of our families trials and tribulations.

At the time Linda's illness was taking up so much of our thought, Randy divorced Phylis. The action was uncontested, and was quickly granted.

Phylis had no schooling or training that would enable her to make a living for herself and our two granddaughters; so we bought a small house for her and the kids in Monmouth, Oregon, where she attended Teachers College. We provided them with enough money to cover monthly expenses.

While Phylis was there she met and married a pony-tailed and "ear ringed" motorcycle biker who was a divorced and defrocked minister.

This was the first time in my "connected family" that I noticed the degradation of males wanting to appear as "she-males", perhaps they would have preferred to be born the opposite sex.

Following their marriage they opened, of all things, a marriage counseling service!

Randy also remarried. His wife Cindi was from a well-to-do Lancaster, Pennsylvania family and was a student at the University of Oregon. Randy met her on the tennis court where he went for exercise while he was taking a course in nursing at nearby Lane County College. He had decided he would no longer be a minister.

When we met Cyndi she was driving a beat up many-colored VW van and was wearing army surplus fatigues.

They lived for a short time on rural acreage in Marcola, Oregon in a cabin Randy had previously built.

Within a year Randy was offered and accepted a position as pastor of the English Presbyterian Church in Marietta, Pennsylvania, a short distance from her folks, against whom she had been rebelling. The only bond with her mother was that of smoking together.

Mary and I provided the Penske rental truck for them to make the move and helped them load it.

Cindi sold the beat up VW van to another "hippie" and drove Randy's new car, which we had recently provided.

Shortly after settling into the manse in Marietta, Cindi was busy raising a little red head named Alison and had little time for anything other. Having a baby was not her thing!

Michael sold the home in Gig Harbor and moved to Ellensburg on the eastern side of the Cascade Mountains where he attempted, with his new wife Elizabeth, to make a living raising black Labrador dogs. This was but another failed enterprise so both he and Elizabeth found work in real estate sales. Elizabeth did quite well and graduated to the level of an escrow agent.

A few years later they moved back to the "wetside" of the mountains to Chehalis, Washington where Elizabeth again went to work in an escrow office. They bought a small acreage nestled in a crook of a river that soon flooded and made a soggy mess of their place.

For a time both worked as substitute teachers in an elementary school.

Mary and I moved off the acreage in Gig Harbor and purchased a condominium in a little wooded glen called Quiet Forest Park.

It was time to enjoy real retirement so we both worked with Bible Study groups and at our church where she did office chores and I did maintenance and construction work.

Chapel Hill Presbyterian Church had become a major part of our lives. I chaired the pastor search and nominating committee that called a young pastor to fill the vacancy left by the long time pastor who felt it was time he left a "church divided".

I did the reconstruction work to provide the new pastor with suitable facilities, and spearheaded the construction of new facilities; chairing the Administration Committee, and then the Building Committee, and helping select and working with the architect.

I enjoyed being a cog in the building of another church.

Mark James Toone soon brought about an amazing growth that made it necessary to expand our classroom facilities and to build an enormous activity center to serve alternately as a full-sized basketball court, and a fellowship hall that seated 400 at dinner. The sanctuary became a chapel as we quickly outgrew it, so we set up chairs, and a platform for speakers and choir, in the new Family Activity Center to seat 500 at each of two services.

Several other volunteer regulars and I dismantled it after the close of the second service and stored the platform sections, organ and piano and all of the chairs so that the area could be used as a gym and basketball court the next morning.

I had been chairman of the Administration Committee and, at another time, of the Outreach Committee. I dropped all other committees to give full time to the Building Committee and later dropped that to chair the Long-range Planning Committee. LRP foresaw the need in the near future of a complete new sanctuary and additional offices and classrooms.

After we had developed the plan for those soon to be required additions I resigned all committee work because of my lack of hearing and of understanding.

I had spent more than $30,000 on hearing aids, but none brought back the needed understanding of words, especially in "group meetings".

Mary continued her activity in Bible Study Fellowship. Since it was held at our church I went with her every week and set up the chairs in the several classrooms occupied by the 200 participating women. I went back at closing time to put the chairs back in the storage room.

With our activities considerably reduced we decided to spend time exploring the interesting places in Washington and Oregon. We never ran out of new places to visit and to explore.

On one exploration we visited the tulip fields in LaConner, Washington. The getting there from Gig Harbor was much more enjoyable when we drove to Port Townsend and boarded the auto ferry to

Whidbey Island from which we could cross a bridge at Deception Pass to the mainland and to the tulip fields.

To keep our travel low pressure we stayed the night at the Best Western Inn at Oak Harbor. The inn is adjacent a restaurant called Mitzels. After dinner we started walking to the motel.

Mary usually held my hand to insure against accidental tripping but this time she held her purse in her hand while I walked alongside.

As we stepped off a small curb she pitched forward without even putting her hands out to break the fall. She went face down onto the concrete. Her chin and mouth were badly torn.

I carried her up to our room and asked the inn operator to call a doctor. She said, "You'll have to take her to the Emergency Hospital in Coupeville, about twenty-five miles south." I said, "Please notify the hospital of our coming."

The doctor on duty cleaned her up and stitched her lip and chin, and recommended I take her immediately to our family doctor in Gig Harbor.

Mary still wanted to view the tulip fields, so I consented to the extent of driving through the area.

While we were driving home on the freeway, every few minutes I would have to straighten her as she involuntarily listed toward me. I knew something other than the cuts and bruises needed caring for.

Doctor Quiring examined her thoroughly and recommended a neurologist. The referral appointment was made and I took her to the neurologist the next day. The neurologist performed a thorough examination, recommended a brain surgeon in Tacoma, and arranged for her to enter St. Joseph's Hospital.

That same day Dr. Michael examined her and reported, "The only way I can ascertain the needed treatment is through drilling a hole in her skull."

As there was no alternative we gave consent.

No evidence was present in the area where they drilled so we were told they had to drill another hole in another area. We gave consent. Again nothing was found so another hole, to be sawed above the left ear, was needed!

Whatever was done in the way of medications and therapy, including the rehabilitation therapy with which I helped, brought her to the place where they allowed me to take her home for about half a day. At home she asked me to do what I could to make the little bit of hair she had left, more attractive. I did the best I could, but since Mary had always been super-fastidious, especially about her hair, it wasn't good.

I took her back to the hospital and continued to help with her rehabilitation. She slowly regained her ability to walk and talk, and to read and write.

Just as I was rejoicing at the progress she was making she suddenly became comatose. I asked the nurse, "What happened." The hospital had a specialist for everything. One specialist was to keep her internal chemistry in proper balance, but he wasn't paying close enough attention to his job. The IVs, her sole nutrition, had gotten her chemistry out of "sync". Her sodium intake was far too low.

The specialist was notified, came in and did some checking, and issued new orders.

The revised formula brought an end to the touch-and-go situation.

After two and a half months of rehabilitation, a group meeting of the doctors and therapist, with the two of us, culminated in a decision that she could go home with weekly visits to the Rehab section.

The next morning when Dr. Michael was to check her and release her he was about two hours late. We were antsy to say the least. He had been in surgery on others into the wee hours of the morning.

When he finally arrived he told us he was releasing her but wanted to make one last withdrawal of fluid for his assurance that all was well.

When he inserted the hollow needle no fluid would come.

Instead of removing and inserting elsewhere as he had always done in the past, he waggled the long hollow needle up and down while still inserted. Her eyes fluttered and she went into a slump and a deep coma!

The shock on Doctor's face jolted me. The doctor and a group of nurses quickly wheeled her to the elevator and down to surgery. I waited in the surgery visitor's room for over two hours. They finally emerged and took her back up to the room. There were no visible vital signs and they hooked her up to life sustaining equipment.

I stood or sat alongside of her, holding her hand, twenty-four hours a day for four days; leaving only long enough to go to the bathroom or to get a quick snack from one of the machines.

If she awoke I wanted to be sure she knew I was with her. On the fifth day I asked Doctor Michael, "Is there life in her or is it only the machines that show life?" He said, "After this long in a deep coma there is no doubt life is gone."

I knew then that actually life was gone four days previous!

I told them to pull the plugs, gathered her few belongings and trudged out like a "zombie".

Although I have no recollection of it, I somehow drove the twelve miles across the Tacoma Narrows Bridge to home in Gig Harbor, to what was now a cold and dreary empty nest.

Mary had given me fifty-two years of trust and companionship and helped me amass a fortune.

We started our life together in a small rental cabin in Compton where we then had our first home built. We lived there sixteen years until I was Executive Vice-president of Pacific Iron and Steel Company; when we built the home in Park Estates and lived in it sixteen years until my retirement, when we moved to the Gig Harbor acreage. Sixteen years later we moved into the Condo at Quiet Forest Park.

We made that retirement move when I was seventy-two.

Until now, sixteen seemed to be a special number in our life together.

Although The Lord provided the wherewithal to do otherwise, in none of our homes or our possessions had our lifestyle ever been ostentatious.

With Mary gone I felt life was over. I let my misery take over and put aside my relationship with the Lord. The loss of Mary was completely debilitating!

I was in a walking stupor and stayed away from everybody, because I was too emotional to face anyone including my kids. I knew I would break down if I tried to talk about the situation.

For a time I was a hermit locked in my little house with the blinds closed. I was no stranger to loss of loved ones but it hadn't prepared me for this. I was, perhaps, the loneliest man on earth.

The loss of Michael's Linda was the prior most difficult. My first loss was that of my Dad when I was six. About five years later we lost Grandpa Sager. Grandpa Logic was next when he died of widespread cancer at ninety-five. Uncle Joe took his own life a few months later, following a most unexpected marriage.

Grandma Sager lasted only a few years after the death of her husband and of her only son.

The next most difficult was that of Dad Straley. Mom and he lived in a Mobile Home Park in Hemet, California. Mom called Mary to tell her about his passing.

I called home from out of town and Mary told me she had just heard from Mom and she and Randy would drive out to be with her. My flight from San Francisco arrived at Long Beach about two hours after my talking with Mary. I walked over to the Hangar where a friend had a charter helicopter service.

In twenty minutes I was in the helicopter and about twenty minutes later I landed within a half block of Mom's home. We spent the day and night with Mom and the three of us drove back to Long Beach.

Mary told me that when the chopper was landing Mom said, "Some idiot is playing around out there with a helicopter". Mary's admitted response, "That idiot is probably your son."

The next loss was Mary's brother Bill. He shot himself through the head while in his car, which he had parked in a remote spot usually occupied by lovers.

The next to go was Mary's mother much bereaved by the loss of her alcoholic son.

Mary was in Spring Valley near San Diego helping Randy's first wife with the birth of Michelle.

"Lil Bittie", as Mary's mom was called, had been ill but assured Mary she was O.K. She was taken to Community Hospital in Long Beach the day after Mary went to Spring Valley.

I visited her, every day for several days, holding her hand and talking with her and kept Mary advised, but assured her there was nothing she could do by rushing back.

"Lil Bittie" passed away, the fourth day, shortly after I left her room.

She had been a loving and delightful lady whose kids, son-in-law, daughter-in-law, and grandkids loved dearly.

Mary's dad immediately remarried and moved to Chico, California; where his new wife had lived for several years with the husband she had lost a few years before.

Pappy, Mary's dad, lived but a few more years and died in Chico. His funeral service was in the church where he and Lucille were very active.

The entire time he had been married to "Lil Bittie" he refused to go to church with her! But he died happy because his new wife introduced him to Jesus as his Savior so that he could live eternally!

That made his quick remarriage more acceptable to Mary and to me.

The next to go was my Mom. Since the passing of Dad Straley, she had lived in her mobile home on my sister Bernice's large acreage in San Marcos Pass, just above Santa Barbara. Mary and I drove up to be with Bernice and to attend the memorial service.

My brother Rolly died in Columbus, Missouri where he had lived for many years with his second wife. His first wife, Emily, had died of lupus, years before. Her funeral was the first service for me that was officiated over by a Rabbi. I had several very good Jewish friends, especially at college, so I felt not too alien in the gathering but the liturgy was certainly different.

I had not seen or communicated with Rolly for many years and did not attend his funeral. I did attend the Elks funeral of my sister Dorothy's first husband Earl. His death came about through the polio that he had before he went to work for me at Pacific Iron. Dorothy remarried and lived in Cave Junction, Oregon. I saw her and her new husband once while Mary and I lived on the acreage in Gig Harbor.

My half brother Larry and his wife Laura lived in Kenai, Alaska for many years but I had not seen or communicated with them for at least twenty. They both smoked and drank quite heavily so we didn't enjoy being around them. However, they were obviously good people because they were well thought of in the community and raised six kids including an adopted Aleut. I might see and recognize them in heaven when I arrive. Both died within twenty-four hours.

They smoked together drank together and died together.

The last death, for which I will be forever thankful, was that of my disastrous "on the rebound" marriage to JR, as I have referred to her ever since my divorce.

The week after the "marriage", she decided to take "the girls" that she worked with in the Rental Real Estate office, "out on the town". Driving the Camry that had been Mary's, she picked them up and hosted them to dinner and libations at one of the shore-side restaurants in Tacoma.

Shortly after midnight, she opened the door to our bedroom, and introduced them to me while I was in bed. I was discomfited by her doing it, and told her so. She took them into the living room where they continued their boisterous behavior for another hour, before she took them home.

She came back home in the wee hours of the morning, and I was displeased; that was perhaps the reason for her later contending to a "marriage counselor", that I was "controlling".

Friends who had been at a Session meeting until about midnight, as they crossed The Narrows bridge, had seen my Camry with a load of women; weaving all over the road, and crossing the center line.

In my attempt to satisfy her, I invested heavily in the "ostentatiousness" that I had previously abhorred. I soon became convinced that it is ruinous to the character of others to make life too easy for them; because they lose incentive to learn and to earn, greedily expecting something for nothing, and never becoming anything.

JR totally fit that picture. She was of the baby-boomer generation that expected to "labor-not" to obtain whatever they wanted, and whose creed was, "If it feels good, do it!"

She was the third boomer with whom I made the mistake of giving too much. Numbers one and two were my sons Michael and Randy. I had given them the maximum allowed without having to pay gift tax, $12,000 a year until it was later raised to $40,000 which Mary and I together gave each couple every year until Mary's death. Additionally I had purchased a $150,000 C.D. for each of the boys, with Mary and me as trustees.

My tax attorney told me I would have to pay gift tax on them, which resulted in a tax payment of $16,800. So, at the date of maturity each of them got $150,000 and I got poorer $316,800 plus attorney fees.

Over the years of their marriages each of them were given $630,000, and both turned against me when I remarried and no more gifts were forthcoming. I relearned that it is totally destructive of character to not allow others to make their own way.

In 1990 and '91 I became involved in several mission activities with friends in our church. My first work mission was in Tijuana, Mexico at the Sparrows Gate orphanage where I repaired a house trailer and prepared it for towing from Tijuana to Tecate.

The orphanage was moving to Tecate because the owner of the Tijuana property found someone who would pay him more than the orphanage could afford. The kids would be far better off because the Tijuana toilet situation was abominable. The stench could be detected from a half mile away.

Dean and Alma, originators of the orphanage, and I towed the mobile home about sixty miles over rutted roads to the new location at Valle de Las Palmas near Tecate, where I then became part of a work crew from Chapel Hill constructing buildings for the new orphanage. We were erecting a building to house the kitchen, laundry room, and dining area. On subsequent trips we constructed dormitory buildings. The temperature was 115 to 125 degrees, and the grounds were literally crawling with tarantulas.

We survived, but more importantly those beautiful big-eyed children were gladdened.

Mid '91 several of us from Chapel Hill church went to Zambia where we linked up with a like number of Christians from North Carolina to make the needed repairs to a hospital in a small and remote village in

Zambia. The hospital was built by Dr.Livingston in the late 1800's, and was much in need of repair.

We worked in 140-degree temperatures in the early morning and late afternoon hours; the coolest times of the day! We ate and rested at midday.

I teamed with a great guy and senior adult friend, Ray Payne. We did all of the plumbing and water line repairs. Since there was no hardware store within a hundred miles, much of our time was spent in unearthing fittings and pipe that had been buried in the dust of the maintenance building dirt floor, and in renovating and installing them in place of those broken or rusted out.

Others of the group did cleaning and painting, and carpentry and cabinet repairs and replacements.

Dr. Livingston had planted two lines of Sycamore trees to form a shady palisade approach to the hospital.

Going from our sleeping quarters to the place of work, we walked in the shade of those trees, until one of the natives told us, "There are Black Mamba snakes in the trees that drop on their victim".

From that time on we preferred the one-hundred-forty degree temperature.

Our cook was a lady from the North Carolina group who did a wonderful job of "nutritioning" us. It was through her that I got re-acquainted with grits, having had them only once before when I was a guest at the Blount's mansion in Montgomery, Alabama.

While I was in East Africa, after completing our three-week mission in Zambia, I flew Zambia Airways to Kampala, Uganda; and experienced "racial prejudice" as the flight steward took care of everyone else, and acted as though I was non-existent.

I had promised an old friend from Uganda who was a Christian minister, and who had established twenty or more village churches, that I would come spend some time with him.

David Musisi was a native of Uganda and had escaped to Kenya when Idi Amin wantonly murdered much of the populace. David's entire family was slain by Amin.

When he returned, after Amin was executed, David buried the remains of his family members in the yard of his father's home.

Those happenings were barely five years before my visit, but much of the evidence of the massacre was still apparent.

David picked me up Friday afternoon at the airport. As I descended the portable stairway, I heard a beautiful sound. A large choir was singing "Amazing Grace". David had one of his helpers drive a big flat-bed truck, on which was about forty people serenading me.

A very stately and beautifully dressed lady met me at the bottom of the stairway and ushered me through customs and over to David's car.

As David drove me to the Kampala Sheraton hotel for a "much needed" rest, I noticed that most of the buildings, some of which were well designed high rise, were gutted and dangerous wrecks!

While on the way he told me we would visit six of the churches the next day for the regular Sunday service. I said, "How long are the services?"

"They are from three to four hours long. The first service will be at about four o'clock in the morning and the last one will be well past midnight."

"How much of that is the sermon?"

"I usually preach from an hour and a half to two hours but that's entirely up to you." "What do you mean, up to me, what have I to do with it?"

"You're preaching, I've told all my churches you were coming and they are awaiting your words from the United States."

"Me preach, I'm no preacher!" "Well you're just about to gain a new title!"

The next morning I asked, "Who is preaching to the other fifteen congregations?" "Seven of them now have pastors and we will drop by today to attend their services.

You are being expected by the people of the remaining eight tomorrow."

David said, "It is often said by persons of a different race that all of another race look alike. That is of course nonsense, however many will look like others you have seen for they will walk many miles to hear you and you will have seen them in one or more of the churches that you have already served."

These dear people were really hungering for the Word; and this neophyte, who had never preached before, had to present a different sermon for each group.

I went to my hotel room about 7pm and, despite having been exhausted from the trip, worked all night to prepare six different sermons.

I had a different interpreter at each church because each community had it's own tribal language. I was so wound up in giving the message, that I forgot to pause for the interpreter to present it to the people. The poor guy had to remember a lot of rhetoric, when I gave him the opportunity to speak.

I spent two weeks with David, and the people who worked with him and lived with him. I saw much of the devastation wrought by Amin's troops and I heard many horror stories.

It was especially saddening to find that all churches and schools were wrecked and the people of each area had gathered the skulls of people of the community and put the unidentified ones in black plastic bags on the church platforms.

David took me out to the world's largest lake, Lake Victoria, where I talked with the fishermen; and told them about Jesus making disciples of several fishermen. I noticed that as I stood on the shore talking with the men that several children had gathered directly in front of me and were staring up at my face.

I thought it was because I'm "colorless", but David said they were entranced by the large amount of gold fillings!

Peter, a friend of David, in that 140-degree climate, wore a knit cap no matter where he went, and had a very bad odor. I inquired of David as to why. He told me Peter was jailed in a small enclosure with many others that perished from Amin's troops spraying mustard gas on them. Although Peter lived through it, the effect was the making of an ever-open and draining wound that rotted his scalp.

Peter's only help was available from a London doctor but they had no means of paying him or of paying for the air travel from Kampala to London and return. I talked with the doctor on the telephone and told him I would pay his fee and the cost of transportation and housing.

Two weeks after I arrived home in Gig Harbor I heard from the doctor and sent the funds. I never heard more about the matter but assume that all went well.

When I flew from Kampala to Nairobi to board the plane for my return to Seattle I had the thrill of watching Jetways being installed there!

I thanked The Lord for giving me Joshua as my role model and giving me John 3:16 as my sermon basis, and Matthew 28:19 "Go, and teach all nations" as my impetus.

It had been a saddening but fulfilling mission.

I felt that I had experienced, "A little walk with Jesus".

A few months later I joined another mission group from Chapel Hill and spent a week in Moses Lake, Washington where the temperatures almost match those of East Africa.

We were upgrading the housing for the migrant workers who work the vegetable crops. Many were the same as our Chapel Hill Zambia missionaries.

My third mission trip was to Jamaica with a work group who would repair and update the facilities of a Bible College called "Christ for the Nations", where many young people from Haiti and Cuba were being trained for Christian ministry.

Naturally I paid for JR and myself, but also paid for her daughter Tina and Tina's husband Jim.

Having just been unintentionally instrumental in getting them out of Jehovah's Witnesses; satisfying JR's desire, I felt the Christian mission activity would help them; and it might help me with JR.

I purchased in Tacoma, and air freighted to Jamaica, two copper tubing coils that I installed on the roofs of the student dorms to give them solar heated water for bathing and for washing clothes.

It was at least 140 degrees on the roofs where I worked the entire time I was there.

It seemed to "fall my lot" to do mission work in the world's hot spots.

Having had had two bouts with heat stroke, I was supposed to steer clear of such environs.

The "climatic" heat was nowhere as debilitating to me as the four years of abasement from JR, through being completely rejected by her!

Why couldn't I see this was a flawed yoking and would never be a real marriage?

I should've ended it quickly, but put it off time and again figuring, "With additional giving on my part she will come to accept me."

After the wedding, her daughter Tina told me that her mother had been previously married four times and two of the husbands committed suicide, also that her mother had gone through a bankruptcy action just before she met me. That information beforehand might have made me wary, but it came too late.

I finally decided to take my pastor's and my lawyers advice.

On August 13, 1994 my attorney filed petition for dissolution. The marriage was almost four years old and I had discussed filing, with my attorney, at least four times.

She wanted to take back the name of her most recent "ex" who, during the early days of our marriage, she proclaimed to her daughter Tina while we were together in my car, "I'll see any time I want!"

She also said that when she found he was sleeping with another woman she just grabbed her personal belongings and left. She asked nothing of him although he was the transgressor and although he owned a hardware store in South Seattle; yet she wanted everything from me after coming into the "marriage "a bankrupt", and with whom the marriage was never consummated!

Having been the bookkeeper for a commercial realty firm, I felt she could handle the bookkeeping and paying of bills, so I never "checked up" on her.

She had made out three checks, on the account that I had when we married, depositing a total of $10,000 in three bank accounts in her name only. I was not aware of it until I was digging through the records to satisfy her attorney; who, paid for by me, kept asking for financial details that he hoped would disclose hidden assets they could grab.

The constant pressure of having to pour over old records including those that related only to my deceased wife and me, and to the tax equivalency trust in her name, had me constantly agitated. Fortunately I had moved all my records into the downstairs apartment, where I resided a year and a half until the dissolution was granted.

I had put the house on the market in February '94 because she wanted to buy a property between her daughter's place and that of her recently released rapist son, but I didn't intend to live next-door to a rapist.

I find nothing more cowardly and despicable than a rapist; except that of a father who sexually molests a daughter and some times even buys the daughter's denial.

"Providentially" she had used up all my available funds including borrowing on my life insurance, so there was no money and none would be available until we sold the Gig Harbor Victorian mansion, which I had built to her desires.

It had 7600 sq. ft., and an indoor swimming pool, spa, steam room, five bedrooms, a huge living room, and a den and game room. From the upper rooms and decks there was a beautiful view of Colvos Pass up to snowcapped Mt. Baker.

Watching the pods of Orca whales from our upper deck was truly awe-inspiring; but even more "awe inspiring" was that I spent over $1,500,000 on the mansion, and JR wanted half of it and half of the bank accounts and Certificates of Deposit, none of which she had any part in providing.

I had to keep the mansion and grounds in excellent condition for the real estate agent to be best able to market it. It was costing me $20,000 a year for taxes, utilities, insurance and upkeep; and was a ten-hour a day chore of hard work.

After a long wait, and three different Realtors over a three-year period, I sold it to a nice orthodox Jew for one third of what it cost me!

The only thing Ethan Golf wanted to change was the metal sculpture of the Christian fish symbol atop one of the three rotunda roofs. It became a Star of David.

The daytimes of physical work were followed night after night with the pouring-over of the files and separating of documents to answer her attorney's demands; that kept me up until 2:00 to 3:00am every morning. I was in a perpetually tired and frantic state. It was all this 77 year-old could handle.

Before I filed, continuing abasement came from her having her kids and grandkids at the house day after day, for evening meals and family sessions that pointedly excluded me. She made it apparent in so many ways that she had no desire to ever put me first in her life, including a bombastic statement in the presence of her daughter, son-in-law and two granddaughters, that she "Never had been and never would be my lover, friend, or companion!"

My only other experience was with a dear sweet woman who gave me 52 years of trust, love, and companionship and helped me save a goodly fortune.

JR single-handedly, in just three and a half years, purloined to her advantage more than $1,000,000.

Some went to pay off her considerable debts and some to help her kids, but most of it she spent, or squirreled away for herself.

After a year and a half of waiting for the trial to be scheduled, I was a basket case. We ended up before an elderly retired judge, who was called in because of an unusually heavy trial load on the Pierce County courts. He took a liking to her display of feminine wiles and to the fact that she had property in an area of Eastern Washington where his daughter lived.

While her attorney and my attorney and I stood before him in the courtroom he engaged her in a friendly chat.

After a few minutes of the chummy patter between them I knew I couldn't come out any better than the pay-off suggested by her attorney. I bought it and walked away without even getting an allowance for the fees I had to pay her attorney; because she didn't have money of her own.

The court wasn't interested in how much it cost me, or how unfair the settlement!

The court system for making divorce judgment, at least in Pierce County, Washington, needs a drastic overhaul: All pertinent documents provided by both parties, as to monetary matters, such as source of funds, should be audited and taken into account in making a settlement.

Also statements as to behavior should be taken into consideration and, if there is disparity, both parties should be given a lie detector screening to determine which is factual.

With these reports in hand, an auditor should recommend the settlement and the judge dispense it!

Perhaps there's too much common sense in that, because it didn't happen. Wrong or right, good or bad, nothing but the judge's whimsy made the decision. She was my Delilah, I her Samson.

We're always vulnerable when outside the Lord's protection zone. Samson lost his sight and might. I lost my right to that which God allowed me to acquire.

I survived only because I was finally back to seeking His will.

In escaping the drudgery of living until the finalizing of the divorce, I planned a trip to Apache Junction, Arizona.

I had been invited to spend time with Phil and Helen Roth, very dear friends from Gig Harbor who had been most supportive of me in my marriage trials.

As I looked over the map to plan my route from Gig Harbor to Apache Junction I noticed I would go through Kingman, Arizona. Virginia Kuzee and her husband Harold, both of whom Mary and I had known at St. John's church, had lived there for some time, in a mobile-home park.

Virginia and Mary had been best friends and faithful correspondents for many years, to the extent that she probably knew more about me than I did. Mary had told me of Virginia having to give Harold the kind of care one would give a small child, because of his disability from emphysema.

Thankfully, Harold was a God loving man and he and Virginia did mission work among the deprived of Cuba and Mexico, and on New Mexico and Arizona Indian reservations.

However, he had a tendency to denigrate his wife.

He had been a heavy smoker and suffered from emphysema for many years. Virginia's lot had again become that of serving others as she nursed Harold through years of his disability, while putting up with his habit of putting her down.

Mary and I knew the load on Virginia was great and wanted to do anything that would help, but she was an "I'll do it myself." individual.

After Mary's death I took to occasionally writing them. I called to ask if I could drop by on my way to Apache Junction. Virginia answered the telephone and I identified myself and asked how Harold was doing. She said he had passed away just a few weeks before. I expressed my condolence and said, "Is there anything I can do to help?" "No".

Shortly after I hung up I thought, "Why didn't you ask to be allowed to stop by, she might need someone to talk with?" I called back and asked if it would be OK for me to do so. She was hesitant and said that she was going to be with her daughter.

With a strong desire to be of help. I asked, "Would it be OK if I stopped by for a short time, on the night that I will be returning through Kingman?" She hesitantly agreed.

I checked into the Best Western in Kingman the evening of return and, following her instructions, went to find the mobile home she lived in.

It was dark and unfamiliar to me so I stopped in front of the mobile about two doors away. As I started up to the door I noticed there was someone else's name on it.

I backed up a few spaces, still confused, when someone stepped out on the front porch. I said, "I'm looking for Virginia Kuzee." The response in that beautiful Mississippi-drawl was, "You've found her."

I will forever cherish those words in the voice I hadn't heard in the more than twenty years since Mary and I last saw her! She invited me in.

As she filled me in on the loss of Harold I hugged her to show my support. When I finished hugging her we stood there just looking at each other. She said, "What shall we do now?" Both of us feeling somewhat awkward I said, "Let's do that again."

That broke the ice and we reminisced awhile and made plans for the next day to tour nearby resort areas and become reacquainted.

We were both amazed at the ease of companionship and openness we shared. What began as just being supportive of each other soon blossomed into planning marriage. Nevertheless Virginia kept telling me of acquaintances that "would be better for me" until I said, "Knock it off you're the only one for me, and since the Lord planned it this way don't talk to me anymore about someone else."

Virginia had organized, and was the continuing prod for, a group of Kingman women in a daily walk around a large park area nearby. I walked with them. After the walk she tried to convince me, one by one, of this one or that one being a better choice for me than she. She was working hard to evade me. I might have easily gotten the impression that she was not at all anxious to marry me!

To get me to further think out the matter she said, "What do we have in common?" "You'd be surprised how much we have in common".

We have both been very surprised. It's, "Do you remember this?" and "Do you remember that?"

While I was in Apache Junction and in Kingman, JR gathered her kids and friends together to remove the many possessions I had purchased, including the antiques that I had restored with painstaking care, and carted them away. She even took the shower curtain that was on the oval shaped rack above the antique tub in the antique bath!

She also took the washer and dryer, the 27" TV that was on the swing arm in the master bedroom, and all the Oriental rugs; all of which were to be sold with the house.

All in all, she removed belongings for which I had paid over $120,000.00, and into which I had put hundreds of hours of hard labor, to restore.

But I put all of that behind me and found it heavenly to be on cloud nine! I had plumbed the depths but now was soaring like an eagle.

On September 27, 1995 (one year and one month after filing for divorce, following five years of rejection), my life was sudden upgraded from "rotten" to "very good"! The divorce was granted.

The Lord heard my plea and provided Virginia Paseur Kuzee, (one year and two months younger than me) as my wonderful, caring sharing loving and God loving, sweetheart, companion and wife.

The tremendous contrast between Mary and Virginia, and JR, was evident in all ways, but especially interesting in the matter of thriftiness.

Mary never spent more than was necessary, JR spent recklessly although she had no part in earning or saving.

Virginia clips coupons and price and value shops, even on small cost items. I learned from her that the old adage, "A penny saved is a penny earned", was filled with wisdom.

I joined her in the pleasure of clipping coupons and seeking bargains, and will now even stoop to rescue a lost penny.

I learned from her that, while I was in Alhambra wrecking a house for twenty-five cents an hour; she was in Mississippi picking cotton, with bleeding fingers, for twenty-five cents for a whole days effort; she was determined to have the money to attend nursing school and become a registered nurse!

Having studied scripture since early childhood she had already adopted the spirit of the good Samaritan.

Virginia and I enjoy discussing the years that Mary and I and Harold and she knew together, and reminiscing about the days of dating between Genna Sue and my younger son Randy.

Randy and Virginias step-kids Harva, Margaret, and Neil had also been good friends.

I had known and enjoyed them as kids in our church high school group. Virginia's stepdaughter Harva (now mine also) and her family have been the very best of kids and grandkids that anyone could ever expect to inherit.

Virginia's memory is far better than mine; however, because she wasn't present to know of it and I wasn't sure Mary had shared it with her, I told her of one embarrassing but laughable incident:

Mary and I had been sponsoring the college age group at St. Johns Presbyterian Church and were with them at a swim party at the Palos Verde home of one of our prestigious members.

Our pastor, Bruce Kurrle, and I were standing near the pool talking when a young man came over to me and said something with someone's name in his remark. My hearing was already in a deteriorated state but I wasn't fully aware of it. My response was, "Never heard of him". Mary overheard the exchange and came over to us and said, "Honey the young man is introducing himself."

Imagine my chagrin. What a way to a friendship!

Virginia's knowledge of what had been going on in my life made us even more bonded. She is the most totally real person I have ever known.

The only things of any import in my life, that she did not know, followed the happening of Mary's hospitalization; and I knew little about her life with Harold except that which she wrote to Mary, but I did know it was rigorous.

Although Harold was not physically injurious to her, as was her first husband, his continual demeaning and the load of caring for him physically was heavy even for a dedicated and extremely strong diminutive nurse.

Neither Virginia's life nor mine was ever "easy come, easy go". We had both worked long and hard to reap, to keep, and to make available, to our church our kids and others in need, that which we gathered.

Neither of us, at any time, was given or inherited anything. We gained what we had because we worked hard to earn it and got the benefit of staying slim and trim.

Now in our little condo home in Boulder City, Nevada, her husband appreciates everything about her, including the diminutive body.

Virginia managed her harvest well, but I got out of step with the Lord, and mine went quickly in the hands of the strange woman, with the spiky apricot colored hair that had black roots.

The two closest Gig Harbor neighbors, who had previously told me they often heard her cussing me in the language of a drunken sailor, described to me the frantic efforts of JR and her crew; while I was in Kingman.

"They were rushing to get everything out and away before your return. They cleaned it out like an overdose of Epsom salt!"

My sin was not only in easy spending, but also in being naive and mulish! I was so bent upon pleasing JR that I put aside listening to and pleasing the Lord.

My dear friend and pastor, Mark Toone, tried hard to convince me, first that I shouldn't marry and later that I should quickly end it.

My friend and attorney of many years, Dave Gordon, also tried to convince me on several occasions.

I would not listen to either.

I was in dire need of companionship, and totally pig-headed and cared not what anyone thought or said.

But September 27, 1995, when the divorce was finally granted (a year and a half after my filing) I put behind me that "old self".

I had plumbed the depths but now scaled new heights; my dear little Virginia and I were formally united.

We purchased together, and moved our possessions into, our little condo home in Boulder City.

We often go the nine miles to Henderson to shop or to eat, where we have noticed a very troubling trend.

It is apparent that more than birth control is needed, because Earth could only hold one third as many when the "baby boomers" reached "maturity" because they had become the obese three to one majority of the nineties.

In the thirties, circus sideshows displayed freaks weighing over three hundred pounds.

In Henderson, Nevada there is an enterprise called "World of clowns", where there is a lifesize Circus billboard of a woman who weighed 365 pounds. It was obviously not normal then.

OSHA should rule that pants belts must be strength tested to withstand the extreme loads put on them by the overhanging stomach of so many of our citizens.

My score four ended on May 9, 1997 at 1:07am.

Score 5

(1:07am May 9, 1997 thru 1:06+ am May 9, 2017).

Rejoicing years.

With total togetherness Virginia and I read scripture every morning as the perfect beginning of wonderful days.

Together, we purchased our condominium in the paradise of Boulder City; the only place in the United States that had from it's inception, a law specifically prohibiting gambling.

Additionally it is the only U.S. community that is home to the little Pipistrelle bat that keeps the skies clean and clear of flying insects, working every night from sundown to sunup!

If the Lord had not led us here we might have ended up "Hapless in Hesperia", from which we moved Virginia.

From our upper deck the view of beautiful Lake Mead is magnificent. The weather is ideal, as attested by our flower and vegetable gardens, which are a great source of pleasure and of delicious fresh vegetables and fruit. Our back yard is also home to numerous quail, chipmunk, and cotton tail rabbits.

Virginia and I are together in all things. The Lord brought us together to make our latter years the best. We honor that blessing.

Ours is a "togetherness", such as has never been seen!

As we always walk hand in hand, the people of our little community and of our little "non-denominational" Faith Christian Church, refer to us as "The Lovers."

Some evenings while she is sitting in her rocker knitting or tatting I read aloud Odgen Nash. Virginia sometimes puts down the handiwork and takes over the reading, especially some of her favorites like C. S. Lewis.

Before bath and bed time we usually get competitive, either sitting on cushions on the floor of our living room with our feet under the coffee table, or the dining table, playing dominoes!

Our days always begin and end with prayers of thanksgiving and in asking the Lord for leading in every aspect of our life.

Virginia and Mary and I had many friends in common when we were at St. John's Presbyterian Church. Her winning personality has now brought us many dear friends in Boulder City:

Ralph and Alice Godwin live within walking distance and have become important in our life. Colonel Godwin was in Army Intelligence where he sought out information of espionage against our country from the end of WW2 through the "Cold War" days. Alice is an avid quilter and heads a quilting club. Their son Ted and his wife, Andrea, were our initial pastors at Faith Christian.

Andrea was of inestimable help to me when Virginia underwent ortho-pedic surgery for a broken shoulder; after tripping over an out-of-place concrete parking block in the local Von's store lot. It was a terrible case of "déjà vu" for me as I recalled Mary's fall in the parking lot of Mitzel's.

My dear little Virginia will have three titanium screws in her shoulder for the rest of her days, and nearly lost her right arm because of surgical fumbling and sadistic nursing by the surgeon's 6'-1" and 240lb. "pony-tailed" queer young brother.

Andrea stayed with me while I waited out the operation at Lake Mead Hospital.

The senior Godwins looked after Virginia's safety when she had to drive back and forth to St. Rose Dominican Hospital in Henderson where she had taken me when I had to have an emergency operation.

Nancy and Larry Richner symbolize Faith Christian Church, and their kids and their families comprise much of its "backbone"

John and Norma Barth have gone far beyond the call of duty by includ-ing us in several of their family gatherings. We two octogenarians have been treated as loving family.

Kent and Ellon Turner and their son, Bret; and their pretty daughter Jessie; who looked after our little three-year old great-granddaughter, Rachel, when we took them to church with us, are special friends.

All of our Faith Christian folks have been exceptionally supportive of us in our octogenarian physical troubles. They are a delightful group.

We considered Bill Welcome, (president of our deacon's board), and his dear wife Dianne to be our "adopted kids" even before they went the extra mile by listening to me while, for the first time in my life, I performed as a "motor mouth".

They asked me about my background while they dined with us at The Lotus restaurant in Henderson. We had asked them to be our guests and I suggested either The Black Angus or The Outhouse as being favorites of ours. When Bill seemed astonished, I realized I had compounded The Outback and The Roadhouse into a name that no self-respecting restaurant would ever adopt!

Virginia's winning ways also won her a bosom buddy, named Hazel Burtak. What a delightful couple of characters they are in our adults bible study group.

Harry and Pat Murphy, and Pat's mother, Alice, have more recently become dear to us.

When the pastor called the little ones forward for the children's "sermon", Virginia grabbed Harry's hand and the two of them joined the kids on the floor at the front of the sanctuary.

Our Lake Mountain area is ideal for the walking, hand in hand, that we find necessary to good health. Additionally we relax by getting in four or five trips each year to new places and to visit loving relatives. Visiting the two or three "less than loving ones" is no pleasure, but we still thank the Lord for them. The loving number has been greatly expanded for both of us through my grandchildren and "great grandchildren", and through Virginia's namesake granddaughter, her grandson Paul and his wife Renee; and Virginia's step-daughters, step-son and stepson-in-law and their children.

We started our '95 traveling when we flew to Memphis and drove to Ripley, Mississippi.

I wanted to become acquainted with, and get the acceptance of Virginia's brother Elmer and his wife Erna Ruth, and their grown up kids Ellon, David, and Randy.

We were there several days, and on July 4th went to Shiloh and walked through the huge cemetery of each the South and the North. It was a moving experience for the day of celebration of our country's independence, recognizing that all of those men died in fighting for what they felt was protection of their particular independence.

I quickly came to love her brother's wonderful family, and they didn't appear to reject me!

We visited also her sister in Olive Branch, Mississippi. Her niece Frances, Virginia's namesake, was the first for me to meet as she greeted us at the airport when we arrived at Memphis. I have never seen a more beautiful reunion.

We went to Sunday service with Frances, where the pastor gave a wonderful message titled "Your appearance is your testimony". I was in full agreement with the message.

The testimony of the obese is, "lack of hard physical work and of control of what is put in the mouth"!

Wherever I have been with my wonderful little lady I have seen people immediately take to her.

She is a truly special person who has helped me greatly expand my horizons.

I had been a "loner" for the four years before The Lord connected us.

My new "Brother Elmer", Virginia's younger brother, was a Methodist pastor serving three small churches and working night hours in the local Mortuary.

He worked daylight weekday hours planting reaping and maintaining human souls, and with whatever spare time he could find planted, maintained and harvested huge helpings of fresh fruit and vegetables from his garden, and fish from his five ponds.

One of Elmer and Erna Ruth's sons, Randy, is a department manager at a Ripley Super Store. The other, David, was pastor of a large and vital Assembly of God church, in the Ripley area.

Their daughter, Ellon, is the wife of a Baptist pastor who headed the Southern Mississippi Conference at the time of our first visit. Rex Yancey is a great guy who pastors a large church in Pascagoula, Mississippi. I became part of that large wonderful family!

In planning our marriage Virginia and I had a huge dilemma.

Deciding who would officiate at our marriage would require Solomon's wisdom:

The pastor of St. John's Presbyterian in Compton, California, where we went to church for many years remained a good friend and lived in nearby Irvine, California. Virginia's pastor in Kingman, Arizona and my pastor, and adopted grandson, at Chapel Hill in Gig Harbor, Washington, were each dear friends, and my son Randy had his Presbyterian pastorate in Marietta, Pennsylvania. That was dilemma enough but to that we added three pastors in Virginia's family.

After much prayer the Lord provided the only solution. We went to nearby Laughlin, Nevada, in the county of our home to be, and were married in the courtroom by the presiding judge.

Having taken into consideration our ages and past history the speech he made, and the poetry he recited, were perfect.

The six foot six bailiff, who was a handsome guy of about fifty, gave Virginia to be my bride! He was also our official photographer and took a picture of the judge and us, which we will forever treasure; it shows, at the hem of the judge's robe, the Nikes he was wearing!

Although we dislike casinos the only special accommodations in Laughlin are the casino hotels, so we made reservations at the Flamingo where we had a super view room. We enjoyed walks along the Colorado River, which runs alongside the hotel grounds. After an extra-special dinner we read scripture before retiring. We were, and continue to be, amazed at the loving and open relationship that the Lord provides us. As we visited later with our family of pastors, one by one, we received the blessing of having our marriage reconfirmed.

After the honeymoon, we used my Toyota "four-runner" to moved Virginia's possessions, from her place in Kingman to the mobile home that she had intended to live in at Hesperia, California. A short time later we rented a U-Haul truck in Gig Harbor and moved my few remaining possessions to our little condo in Boulder City. This was not the way-to-go for a couple nearing eighty.

On the trip from Gig Harbor we came into Nevada through Idaho at Jackpot. A few miles out of Jackpot Virginia heard a siren. I looked in the side mirror and saw flashing lights. I pulled over so that he could pass and he nosed me into the gravel.

He sat in his patrol car talking on the phone. I got out and went back to talk to him and he said, "Stand right there and don't make any fast moves!"

After standing there for some time while he conversed on the phone he lit into me about being, "A menace and should never have ever been allowed on the road."

In sixty-five years of driving I never had a citation or an accident.

In an under-powered four-cylinder Toyota truck he claimed I was going well over 100 miles an hour, tailgating and cutting in and out of traffic.

Virginia got out of the truck and came back to talk with this savior of the highways. She told him, "He's the best driver I've ever known and has never had a citation or even a warning in his more than sixty years driving."

After raking me over the coals a bit longer he wrote out a ticket costing over $300.00, and trashing my perfect record. What a beautiful official welcoming that was to new residents of the state of Nevada!

As we drove away Virginia said, "You would have thought we were Bonny and Clyde". After I calmed down a bit I said, "You know honey, that guy might have been our guardian angel. He certainly got me to be super cautious! God surely does work in mysterious ways and through strange people."

On our first use of a U-Haul, when we moved Virginia's possessions from Hesperia to Boulder City, the trip went better although we became aware that driving rental trucks, having no regular rear view mirror, is hazardous. On this adventure we had no problems with a self-righteous over-zealous patrolman but we had a little incident when using the pullout aluminum ramp for unloading.

The ramp, contrary to usual equipage, did not have a hook attachment to secure it to the truck bed.

We had successfully unloaded and placed in the house everything except a large coffee table made of 2" thick lumber and weighing about 80 pounds. I had it under one arm and stepped from the truck bed onto the ramp. It parted from the truck and went crashing down. Virginia was standing nearby and reached out a hand to steady me, as I fell with the table under my arm. Had she not steadied me I might have broken a leg, but my concern was that the entire mess might fall on her feet. We lost no time in thanking our Lord for protection as I walked into the house with the table still under my arm and Virginia's hand in mine.

My son, Michael, and I had little or no contact since Mary's passing, but in contact with him by letter and phone to tell him about our marriage he told Virginia, "You are a most welcome addition to the Lodjic family"

We enjoyed being together on several occasions, in our home and in theirs, and when we took him and Elizabeth on the train trip from Williams to the Grand Canyon and on the coach tour of the Canyon.

Randy accepted Virginia most readily since he had known and respected her from his teenage days. We visited him and his family in Marietta, Pennsylvania and they visited us in our Boulder City. Virginia's introduction to Alison, Randy and Cindi's six year old daughter, included getting down on the floor with her in her bedroom and playing with the dolls and doll house. She loves kids and took immediately to our sharp little red head.

I became grandfather to Virginia's grandson and his wife and to her namesake granddaughter and great grandsons Corey, Adrian and Harley.

When Harley was yet unborn, we spent a wonderful day with granddaughter Virginia and the two boys at Sea World in San Diego.

Virginia's grandson Paul and his wife Renee have been with us four times. Renee played basketball on her college team in Fresno, California where she earned her teaching credentials through a scholarship. Paul and Renee accepted me as Poppa Carl, making me feel a part of their family. When we visited them in Fresno we found it had become an armed camp because of out of control lawlessness. We were glad they didn't decide to pursue their teaching careers there.

Michael's daughter Rahna, and her husband Tom have been to us like our own kids. They immediately took to Virginia and show her their love.

When 6'4" Tom first met her and found that she too was a fisher-person he wrapped his big arms around her and said, "You're a keeper!" They visit us whenever possible and we count their little daughter Rachel as a special blessing!

The five of us have vacationed together and found it naught but joy. They are definitely our kids, because I proudly walked Rahna down the aisle and gave her away when she and Tom married. I'm forever thankful that Michael refused to attend the wedding.

We have thoroughly enjoyed "fun times" with all of Tom's family in Gig Harbor. His dad is a commercial fisherman as is Tom and two of his brothers, each with his own ocean going boat and crew.

The other brother, Gary, was a fisherman but settled into a profession of cabinetry when Lori bore the first of their three children.

The dangers of commercial fishing in frigid Alaskan waters do not befit a family man. But the three boats in the family bring in a good living and fishing is what they know and do best.

Being with all of them at a birthday or holiday gathering is delightful because they always make us feel we are much a part of the entire family. When it comes to something like changing a diaper you can't pick out who belongs to whom. They behave as though they and we have all lived happily together for a great long time.

Michael's son Eric and his wife Julie and three wonderful little ones leave no doubt they love their Grandma Nina and their Poppa. Ric and Julie began their marriage wanting a big family. Katey, the oldest, has been a special joy and continues so although Kevin too has taken over a place in our hearts, as has of course my namesake Karlie. Ric and Julie named her Karlie as being the closest to Carl Lewis as possible and yet being very much a special girl's name.

Tom, Rahna and Rachel; and Ric, Julie, Katey, Kevin, and Karlie have all joined us in Boulder City to celebrate our birthdays. What wonderful loving kids!

We are blessed through Michael's refusal to have anything to do with them; as we have been allowed the place of loving parents.

Virginia and my sister, Bernice, first got acquainted on the telephone and regularly correspond. They started their relationship calling each other "Sis", putting a special warm spot in my heart. The two of them are so very alike in their life priorities that the relationship is beautiful to observe. We have visited several times in her Oakhurst, California home where she has a considerable acreage and raises all kinds of produce including fruit and nuts. We three enjoy daily walks around the property perimeter with Bernice' dogs, "Miss Kitty" and "Fritzie"

.

The dogs are necessary to Bernice's safety because her husband is gone most of the time.

Clyde is busy at their old place in San Marcos Pass, about four hundred miles away, doing his thing with junk that he accumulated through the years of their marriage, and bringing truck-load after truck-load home to Oakhurst.

Bernice's has been a different kind of marriage in which the husband takes no responsibility for anything other than his own desires. Clyde never knew the meaning of togetherness. He loved his trash and had no love left over for anything or anyone else. Other than that he's a nice guy, but each piece is a treasure he might someday need.

It truly takes all kinds to make up a world.

Virginia and I started exploring places of interest and getting to know each other's family in the few weeks before we married. We then took care of the moving chores to have our home ready for us when we returned from our honeymoon, on which we flew to Vancouver, British Columbia, where we boarded the Canadian Railway VIA Rail for a trip across Canada to Toronto. From our sleeper stateroom and the Vista-dome car we enjoyed together the beauty of southern Canada. The service and food in the dining car were excellent. The dining car had tables for four so we were always seated with another couple. In that way we got acquainted with many of our fellow passengers.

Virginia is an especially good conversationalist and has such a winning personality that getting acquainted comes easily. One memorable "becoming acquainted" experience came from our being seated at a table with two young women. I asked, "Are you sisters?" They smiled and said, "No". We asked if they were married, assuming that they might have husbands at home who could not accompany them. They said, "Yes". So we asked about their husbands. Their coy response was, "No, we're married to each other".

Virginia is fourteen months my junior and I was nearing eighty, so we could remember how much better our world had been before society started accepting such decadent behavior.

A far more enjoyable conversation was had with a young couple who sat across from us one morning at breakfast. We told them we were honeymooners.

They said, "We're also newlyweds" and that he worked for her father. I asked, "What does your father-in-law do?" "He owns a mortuary".

There were jokes regarding "customer relations", which we all enjoyed.

We finished breakfast and as we were leaving, Virginia said, "I hope you have more children than we". We being octogenarians, all enjoyed a good laugh.

The return trip on Amtrak from Chicago to Seattle was not as pleasant as the VIA Rail, and the food and service was much inferior, but we enjoyed getting out at the many stops and having a brisk walk. Sometimes, at places such as Minot, North Dakota, our summer clothing was not quite adequate but we moved much faster, and survived and enjoyed.

Our next travel adventure was when we took our first ocean cruise, on The Spirit of Alaska. It was a small ship with only 42 staterooms and could get into the small inlets of the Inside Passage of Alaska. Our stateroom had a large double bed, sofa and full bath. The view through our starboard windows was always terrific and we were right next to the forward lounge where we had our times of fellowship, where we got well acquainted with a couple named Wally and Dee Zelinski. They are now dear friends.

As one might guess, with a name like Zelinski, Wally is a fellow Polack. His dad immigrated to the area of Canby, Oregon where he purchased a large acreage which he divided among the five boys, who have planted it in grass seed; a very profitable enterprise.

When later visiting them in Canby, we re-hashed our Spirit of Alaska experience and were much agreed that the entire cruise was the greatest! The calving-off of the glaciers within fifty feet of our bow and newborn seal pups floating by on ice floes, from which their mother was trying to push them, were a joy to behold; as were the eagle flocks of twenty or more and family groups of Brown bear. We saw as many as fifty sea otter playing around on the shore of some small islands. The company, the scenery, and the food were excellent.

We count that experience as one of our extra special moments!

In these years of ripe old age all joyful events are like but a moment.

Another such moment was the visit of Virginia's late husband's cousin, Reverend Paul Zylstra and his lovely wife Sue. We had a wonderful time together with a Lake Mead cruise breakfast and tours of local attractions such as the World of Clowns in Henderson where Virginia and Sue rode the merry-go-round together.

One of the displays is that of the pictures and clothing of a woman clown who weighed 360 pounds, and was therefor a circus sideshow freak. Not many years ago, being ugly with fat was an extreme embarrassment.

The fast food organizations are good for the stockholders, but have contributed greatly to this disabling of many people. Other major contributors are the soft drink manufacturers and the "all you can eat" buffets. Often when you see extremely fat persons you see the bottle of soft drink in their hand. "Diet this or that" benefits only the diabetic.

Being married to the television or the computer also contributes to the fatness of so many of our populace.

Our Surgeon General announced to the press that our country's major health problem was obesity, and that it came from nothing other than over-eating and under-activity.

When Virginia was in the hospital with a broken shoulder the two supervisor nurses on her floor were so obese they couldn't pass one another in the hallways without turning sideways.

No doubt the nurses union will advocate and agitate for wider halls!

It's counter-productive for the labor unions and the liberal elements of our government to deny employers the right to refuse employment to anyone who is extremely overweight, or who is a "she-male" with ear or nose ornaments, long hair, pony-tails or decorated finger nails.

Virginia is the world's best cook, but when we both became octogenarians, I told her that it was time she also got some retirement.

We eat out at selected restaurants three times a week, but avoid restaurants where any personnel are other than fully male or fully female, or are obese; doing our small part in forcing a change of lifestyle for those who are caught up in either "dereliction".

In Y2K, thankfully, obesity has again become a source of severe embarrassment such as it was in the days when such people were displayed as circus sideshow freaks! Obesity specialists claim 2.1 pounds per inch of height is the ideal weight for a man and 1.7 pounds per inch for a woman.

Living in the gambling state we've become aware of a great injustice in the income tax laws. Gambling losses can be offset against income but actual out of pocket loss on the sale of a home cannot. What a travesty of justice, and what a wonderful break for the gamblers and gaming industry.

Another miscarriage of justice is seen in agreements by the State of Nevada to use Nevada public funds to pay for improvement of California highways, leading to the gaming places. In many ways we see annoying bias on behalf of the casinos, such as roads and traffic signals put in only for their convenience, and "sound barrier walls" put up along the freeways to aid the developers! We don't appreciate our "tax dollars" providing extra earnings for "selected interests".

In spite of these Nevada defects, and our governor being soft on sexual deviants, our little Boulder City, with it's no gambling law, and it's emphasis on kids and family, is the Eden of this continent.

Virginia's niece Ellon and her husband Rex, who pastors a large Southern Baptist church in Pascagoula, Mississippi, flew into Las Vegas from Salt Lake City where they attended a convention of their church. We picked them up at McCarran Field and brought them home with us to spend a couple of joyful days together.

Virginia arranged for a dinner cruise on the Desert Princess tour boat on Lake Mead. Although it was a little previous we celebrated Rex and Ellon's wedding anniversary. Their visit brought to mind a comment Rex had made: "Daughters of Methodist ministers make great wives for Baptist preachers."

My "Amen" to that is, the combination makes for the very best of family!

Virginia had almost conquered a long bout of high blood pressure so we decided it was time to do more traveling. We first went to visit my sister, Bernice, but no longer felt up to the long drives by car. We flew from Las Vegas to Sacramento and rented a car for our short drive to Oakhurst. The short drive turned out to be five tiring hours. We stopped in Modesto for breakfast-lunch and then on to her place where we would disrupt her because she always insists on giving us her bedroom and bath.

We had two good days with her. The three of us, and her dogs Miss Kitty and Fritzie, were glad to again be together.

Our next catch up visit was with our Mississippi kinfolk in Ripley and in Olive Branch. We flew to Memphis where we rented a car and spent two nights with Virginia's namesake niece Frances, before driving to Olive Branch. In Olive Branch we checked into the Comfort Inn and went to visit my sister-in-law, Enolia, and her family.

Two days later we drove to Ripley where we stayed with nephew Randy and his wonderful little wife Kristy. While they were at work we spent our daytimes with my brother-in-law Elmer and his wife Erna Ruth. During a couple of evenings at Elmer and Erna Ruth's we were visited by nephew David and his wife Nancy and their two beautiful children Jessica and Joshua. David pastored a large Assembly of God church, and Nancy is star salesperson in a Ripley jewelry store.

Grandniece Jessica was following in her great aunt Virginia's footsteps in studying to be a registered nurse but decided instead to work with church youth. She and Virginia had much to discuss. Josh (Joshua) is still in his teens and enjoying being a basketball star. It was a wonderful reunion.

We stayed home for a short time and then in February of '98 went on a cruise with a large Rotary group from Boulder City, because it would give us the opportunity to know more B.C. citizens.

We flew to Houston, Texas and then boarded the Norwegian Star for a cruise into the channel between Nicaragua and Roatan Island.

The ship had just been recommissioned, after having lost it's license because of a large incidence of sickness among its passengers.

As we were on the return trip from Roatan, a lady passenger became very ill. She was removed from the ship by helicoptor and taken to a hospital in Houston, but deceased enroute.

Both Virginia and I felt queasy, but didn't realize that the "bad" air in our cabin, (the highest priced on the ship, right next to the captain's cabin), and the water being not potable, (but not noted as being so), were the source of our ill feeling.

When we returned Dr. Falvo found Virginia to be suffering, for the first time in her life, from extremely high blood pressure. The medication she was given didn't seem to help, so I suggested that she go to a Boulder City M.D., who prescribed a heavy dosage of potassium. She got much worse, so we switched to Dr. Kessler, who told Virginia that her potassium level was so high that she could drop dead any moment; and changed her prescription.

It was a long battle but she got enough better for us to make additional little trips.

I was also feeling rather "out of sorts" so I had Dr. Kessler check me. After his X-ray department photographed me, he told me that I had pneumonia, and prescribed the proper medication.

I got over it, but shortly after had another bout. These bouts of pneumonia were pre-cursor to my hospitalization for an extended period for urine backing up against my kidneys.

My poor little Virginia was put to a lot of anguish as I was put through hospitalizations and operations to correct the problem.

Dr. Kessler made an appointment with Dr. Qazi, a renal specialist, to see us in Boulder City as neither of us felt capable of driving outside of Boulder City.

Dr. Qazi examined me and scheduled an operation on my prostate by Dr. Kaplan, in our wonderful Boulder City Hospital.

The surgery crew, doctor, anesthetist, and nurses gathered in the operating room. Dr. Kaplan agreed with my dear little Virginia that with such hard and frequent hiccups they could not operate.

To the disgust of the surgery crew, the operation was called off. Dr. Quasi referred me to Dr. Suvakumar, a gastroenterologist at the St. Rose Medical center in Henderson, who found and removed small tumors in my colon and esophagus.

The hiccups that had worn me to a mere 132 pounds stopped, and I no longer suffered allusion of objects being thrown at me and of voices yelling at me.

Virginia pampered me to the point of feeling steady on my feet, being able to go for daily walks, and regaining my weight. What a wonderful, wonderful little sweetheart and nurse she is!

Our next trip took us, and our guests, Paul and Sue Zylstra, to Maui in Hawaii where we spent eight days enjoying the tropical water and exploring the best of our fiftieth state. The beginning of this adventure was not at all pleasant. We had decided, because of partial walking disability, to make use of the volunteer wheel chair service.

Sue was in the leading wheelchair. Although Virginia had given her their tickets ahead of time, she mistakenly told the volunteer we were flying America West. All four raced across the garage and across the road to the America West departure wing.

When I realized what was happening I told my volunteer we were leaving on Delta flight 1615 to LAX, and then connecting to Delta 1565 to Kahului, Maui.

The four volunteers with their passengers raced across the street to the monorail that would take us to the Delta wing. We made a last minute boarding with four exhausted volunteers seeing us off.

This resembled a Three Stooges movie!

Delta 1615, a Boeing 767, raced down the takeoff runway and a malfunction (or the flight engineer hitting the wrong switch) triggered pressurization.

I had a bad cold when we boarded, and the improper pressurization made my head feel as though it would split open, I started bleeding from my nose and ears and spent the rest of the Maui vacation in misery. I was not alone in feeling the discomfort, everyone on the flight experienced extreme discomfort, but mine was possibly more intense because of my cold.

Kahana Shores had a brown pea-gravel beach, so none of us enjoyed it the way we would if it had been clean white sand.

Virginia, falling into her usual nursing role, took excellent care of me, and spent much of her time making me comfortable. She and Sue spent some time chatting and shopping while Paul reworked this manuscript.

More recently we did a delightful "de'ja'vue". We retraced the steps of our marriage: the drive to Laughlin, the night in the Flamingo, the river walks, the trip over to the court house, and even a delightful discussion with that handsome 6'6" bailiff. He remembered us from five years previous and had anther big hug for Virginia and another congratulatory handshake for me. We added in a movie at The Riverside casino, titled Anna and the King. it was wonderful.

Virginia and I have gathered many "keepsakes"; the most dear to us are beautiful letters, from two beautiful grand-daughters, expressing great love for the two of us. The first came from our grand-daughter Rahna, the daughter of my son Michael, who abandoned me and his children:

"Dear Papa and Nena; Just a note to let you know how very special you are to me and my family. Words don't seem to do justice when it comes to how we feel. But, I'll try: When I think of you, I think of love. The love you share with each other and the love, wisdom, and grace you share with us.

Your unconditional love has meant more to me than you will ever know, You constantly give us a wonderful example of faith, love, companionship and compassion with a little humor and lots of laughter thrown in. There is so much I have learned from you and there is so much more to yet learn!

I love you for the wonderful people you are. You are family and give me a sense of belonging. For that I am so grateful. I am blessed to have people in my life that see me just as I am, and still accept and value me. Thank you for all that you are and will continue to be. And so, I hope that some day you will call me when you are down or need help; so that in some way I can give to you a part of me, just like you have given me parts of you! I love you. Love Rahna"

The other came from grand-daughter Virginia Lee; the daughter of Genna Sue; who wants as little as possible to do with her mother and me.

E-mail from Virginia Lee:

"Subject; Attn: Carl but grandma can read also.

I just want to tell you, that before reading about your life, I had a lot of love and respect for you, mostly because of the way you have loved and taken care of my grandmother. She has had a tough life. There were times, that I wanted to snatch her away from Grandpa Kuzee, because of the way he treated her; like she was his slave, so was expected to do for him the things she did; not recognizing that she did them because she is a most unselfish person.

I am so grateful to you, and to God, for bringing you into her life. I know you make her happy.

Now, after reading your book, I have learned just what you are made of, and have even more respect for you. I know that the book will be an inspiration to all who read it.

I am glad that you are in grandmother's life and am grateful to have the chance to know you.

Love: Virginia Lee."

Another keepsake is a letter I received from a lady, new on church staff at Chapel Hill Church in Gig Harbor, telling me that many times she has heard, "Carl Lodjic did this", or "Carl Lodjic did that", when someone remarked about some feature at the church.

Each of us also has our private collection of the letters and cards from each other during the days of our courtship.

Now, in this last score of years:

When we are not traveling we go to Henderson, just nine miles to the West where we dine at Sweet Tomatoes, and browse Barnes and Noble's Bookstore from where we have acquired a considerable library.

The homelike atmosphere is so comfy that we have a cup of Starbucks coffee while we quick scan new books to take along on our travels; for the times when there is nothing to be seen out the windows.

With the 2YK phobia ended, we decided it was time for us to go to the Caribbean Sea for some warm water swimming. Virginia and I flew to Atlanta and on to St. Johns in the Virgin Islands. We prefer to travel by air because long term sitting is difficult for octogenarians, and is even then uncomfortable if the configuration doesn't provide a two-seat section, otherwise one of us might be miserable from an overweight person pouring-over from an adjoining seat.

We took the little shuttle ferry from St. Thomas to St. Johns where we settled in for ten days of thoroughly enjoying the life of beach bums. If there are two Paradise on earth Boulder City is one and St. Johns the other.

We thoroughly enjoy the beautiful National Park that comprises most of the Island of St. John. The entire island is a gift to the American public from Lawrence Rockefeller who owned it for several years. We use the little commuter ferry to visit St. Croix and St. Thomas. St. Thomas is a shopper paradise but we are mostly "lookers" because we concluded years back that having things is only a nuisance if you have the necessities already in your possession.

St. Johns' is free of the people problems that most urban areas face with wanton defacing, destruction, and mayhem. Here, looking crummy is not the in thing, we don't even see kids wearing pants with the crotch down between their knees or with disgusting looking haircuts, or "she-males" with long hair or ponytail or ear ornaments, having wanted to be born female! Nor do we see guys and gals with backward facing sport caps!

In all of our travels we have never found more acceptable inhabitants or more beautiful beaches, and so desirable a climate and environment.

By mid '2000 the rejection of the obese became so strong that many took part in a nationwide regimen of exercise, and of eating and drinking only enough to sustain themselves. Some came to realize that Diet Coke or Diet anything didn't keep them from adding blubber.

But the airlines charging by the pound, and the Surgeon General's announcement that obesity was our primary health problem, helped hasten this change for the better.

Although they preferred the lack of hard work and disliked a regimen of no sweet drinks and no alcohol, and of eating only fresh fruit and vegetables, they found it made them more of what used to be "normal".

With obesity on the wane the time may soon come when this fallout from the baby boomers has come to an end. Their discovery of the joy in being real people, through physical activity and sensible eating, has finally sunk in. Many have dieted but many more have simply "died of it"!

October 29, 2009, Virginia and I found we had survived Y2K with hardly a ripple, but those who owned stocks felt a crash that far outstripped '29.

The lawlessness that followed caused our authorities to enact laws providing for mandatory life imprisonment for murder, crippling or proven rape, with no possibility of parole.

New laws also provide for automatic jailing for 39 days for proven defacing, by graffiti or otherwise, and for proven littering.

Exceeding the posted speed limit brings a jailing of one day for each mile per hour in excess of the limit, no excuse accepted!

Enforcement is aided by long range day and night cameras, which automatically zero in on illegal activity. Thousands have been installed in safe boxes to record any such lawlessness. Photo images are transmitted direct to Police Headquarters and to the evidence file. There is no other evidence necessary for jailing without recourse, resulting in elimination of courtrooms and personnel.

Tax moneys from the law-abiding public are no longer squandered on the defense of the criminal. Valuable court time and space are no longer taken up. Hallelujah, public funds are at last being used to improve life for the law abiding!

Virginia and I returned to St. Johns for another visit but this time we decided to extend the time and become involved with a totally ecumenical Christian church, fully sect and color blind!

We are double tithing our time as well as our funds and enjoying every part of it! Being fully accepted and loved by people of color, (yellow, brown, red, black or whatever) and by the "colorless" as well, gives us a warm feeling.

Grand children and great-grand-children make an annual pilgrimage to spend time with us here, and we make an annual wintertime visit to Boulder City to be with dear friends and family who can't afford time or money to see us at St. Johns.

Colin Powell finally acceded to be available for The Presidency and won by the greatest ever majority! Al Gore was again the has-been Democratic Party candidate.

Under Powell's leadership a coalition of Christian countries eliminated Saddam Hussein, who I have long referred to as "Sadamn ol shame".

The National Education Association has been dismantled and our country has resurgence of "teaching excellence" and of following Christian principles.

Global order is now fully stable with the Palestinian situation finally peaceful.

The children of Israel have the land God promised to Abraham, Isaac and Jacob; and Yasir Arafat was assassinated by a group of his own followers! All things are readied for the day of the Lord's return.

Virginia and I are readied for leaving Planet Earth, by having paid for each of us to be cremated and our ashes mixed together and scattered either in the desert near Boulder City or in the sea off the shore of St. Johns.

We expect to be transported together, hand in hand, to be with God from either St. Johns or Boulder

City so we're doubly glad we don't have the obesity problem. We won't put extra stress on the angels.

Postlude: (Prophesy)

I became a centenarian May 9, 2017 at 1:07+am.

For all our years together we beseeched the Lord to take us into His house, hand in hand, when we both reached 100. I waited fourteen months for Virginia.

July 11, 2018, on our patio, rocking together in our rocker built for two, we were taken up as the Lord promised.

Settling in for eternity, we planted our flag on top of Zion where we bask in the light of God's countenance aware that there is no Jew and Gentile, no black and white. All are translucent with God's light shining through.

With front row tickets we await the concert in which Grandpa Sager and our dear friend Paul Zylstra will present a heavenly violin duet.

If you are reading this from Planet Earth you may yet have a last chance. Pass the entry test by coming to know Jesus as your Lord and Savior before Earth's final day, and you will beat the heat.

The author is working on a sequel; although fully aware potential readership has been greatly reduced to the few persons comfortable enough to curl up with a book.

Not even an asbestos book would withstand the temperature of the overcrowded other place! Check with your favorite celestial bookseller or E-mail *vircarlojic@Lord's* place, for an update.

Amen and Amen!

www.ingramcontent.com/pod-product-compliance
Lightning Source LLC
Chambersburg PA
CBHW020245290526
45784CB00003B/1107